MISSOURI

Lost Gold, Hidden Hoards and Fantastic Fortunes

10 LOST TREASURES: Missouri

Commander - J. Hutton Pulitzer, CC, CSA, CSI, ACE

Cover Design and Book Layout by Christopher Cline

Table of Contents

Chapter One... 1

HISTORY HUNTERS OR HISTORY LOOTERS?

Chapter Two 7

"FROM THE MOUTHS OF BABES".

Chapter Three...15

THE PRIVATELY FUNDED TREASURE HUNT THAT STARTED IT ALL!

Chapter Four.. 27

MILLIONS, BILLIONS, OR TRILLIONS?

Chapter Five... 33

CACHEOLOGY

    CACHE OF CEREMONY...36

    CACHE OF CONVENIENCE..36

    CACHE OF CATASTROPHE..37

    CACHE OF DURESS 38

    CACHE OF CRIMINAL ACTIVITY 39

    CACHE OF NATURE...40

Chapter Six... 43

FILL IN THE BLANKS AND FIND YOUR FORTUNE!

    C IS FOR CONSOLIDATE...50

    A IS FOR AUTHENTICATE...55

    C IS FOR CULL...56

    H IS FOR HISTORY 58

    E IS FOR EXPLORE 59

Chapter Seven 61

HOW TO BUILD YOUR PERSONAL TREASURE CASE FILES

Chapter Eight 71

CASS COUNTY HIDDEN TREASURE

Chapter Nine 91

ALF BOLIN

Chapter Ten 111

BONE HILL

Chapter Eleven 131

COPPER AXE CAVE

Chapter Twelve 151

QUANTRILL'S RAIDERS

Chapter Thirteen 171

VALENTINE'S DAY GOLD

Chapter Fourteen 191

LIVINGSTON LEAD

Chapter Fifteen 211

LOST BUCKET OF GOLD

Chapter Sixteen 231

FRED'S FARM CACHE

Chapter Seventeen 251

A DOCTOR'S BETRAYAL

CHAPTER ONE

HISTORY HUNTERS OR HISTORY LOOTERS?

Artifact Rescuers or Archaeological Racists?

"Could imagine nothing pleasanter than to spend all of our lives digging for relics of the past"
-Heinrich Schliemann

Controversy is boiling around the term "Treasure Hunter" or "Treasure Hunting". Regularly I get into online group debates over the use of the term "Treasure Hunter". It actually sickens me to see people arbitrarily classify the two words "treasure hunter" as a "grave robber" and as something illegal. Personally, I liken the term "looter" to the term "racist" and here is what I mean by that.

In the Archaeological community people have been trained to scream "looter" at anyone who is treasure hunting, history hunting, metal detecting or artifact collecting. The reason they scream "looter" is because it tends to put people immediately on the defensive and it gives the one screaming "looter" the upper hand because they then control the conversation, debate and/or discussion (although there is very little discussion and mostly screaming and drowning out by those yelling "looter"). The exact thing happens when someone calls another person "racist". They immediately put the other party on the defensive and in most cases all one can do is start to back off from their position and immediately start apologizing. In other words, calling someone a "looter" or a "racist" is a word used to shut people up immediately or force an apology or backing off from their position, with no regard if the actual position has merit to begin with.

As for me, when that word is "screamed at me online" (I say that because it is usually a single post of that word is in **ALL CAPS**, which is the online equivalent of yelling at someone), very often, but in my usual style I do not back off and always answer every accusation with compelling facts supporting my stance. Invariably more often than not, the group admin – who is most likely an academic involved in the Archaeological community clicks that virtual button to shut me up. What is that virtual shut-someone-up button? The "Ban from Group" button. By banning one and shutting down debate or discussion, they feel doing such gives them the last word. They almost always continue on in the group among themselves bashing me and all treasure hunters and there is not a thing we can do to rebut the accusations. Thus the cycle of misinformation continues to dig deeper into the overall consciousness.

Sometimes, and not the norm at all and not more of an actual end result of more than 1% of all these online debates (or debates against the counter opinion of the group), the group will actually find a mutual ground with me – a horrible Treasure Hunter or History Hunter – and they agree to disagree but let the participation in the group continue. That is the way it should be, since freedom of speech is something to be cherished, supported and honored; if not for it being the right thing to do but the honorable thing to do in honoring the millions in history who have fought wars and died for this basic right. Freedom of Speech.

Here is how I usually fight this fight head on and at least stimulate a helpful and healthy debate of the issue of whether one is a "History Hunter" or "History Looter" an "Artifact Rescuer" or an "Archaeological Racist".

What has happened is the archaeological community has forgotten and shunned its roots (something I deal with as a Jew and the Jewish people shunning their roots and hating everything Jewish, but that is another topic all together). The system has turned on itself and started to devour itself, but has not come out the other end and totally reinvented itself yet. The inevitable "Phoenix rising from the ashes". There is a "reinvented solution" (I will share it a few chapters forward) that already exists today for this problem; but here in the United States this "reinvention" has not occurred yet and unfortunately the result is both hard to interpret laws and laws with unintended consequences (or intended consequences depending which side of the debate you come down on).

This cycle has a symbol and the symbol is called the "Ouroboros".

The Ouroboros or Uroboros (/jʊərəˈbɒrəs/; /ɔːˈrɒbɔrəs/, from the Greek οὐροβόρος ὄφις tail-devouring snake) is an ancient symbol depicting a serpent or dragon eating its own tail.

Often symbolizes self-reflexivity or cyclicality, especially in the sense of something constantly re-creating itself, the eternal return, and other things such as the phoenix which operate in cycles that begin anew as soon as they end. It can also represent the idea of primordial unity related to something existing in or persisting from the beginning with such force or qualities it cannot be extinguished. While first emerging in Ancient Egypt, it has been important in religious and mythological symbolism, but has also been frequently used in alchemical illustrations, where it symbolizes the circular nature of the alchemist's opus. It is also often associated with Gnosticism, and Hermeticism.

So to understand both the problem and the "solution to and of" the "History Hunter" versus "History Looter" or "Artifact Rescuer" versus "Archaeological Racists" we have to go back in time and understand the beginnings of an industry first.

CHAPTER TWO

"FROM THE MOUTHS OF BABES".

An industry built from the imagination and determination of an 8 year old who loved books!

"My sole and only aim is to be able to establish a historical fact, on which I disagree with some eminent historians and geographers"

-Heinrich Schliemann

What a lot of hobbyist do not know and most academic professionals choose to ignore, is that the profession and educational institution of Archaeology all began with (insert dramatic drum roll here) a "History Hunter" who was ultimately called a "History Looter", who was really an "Artifact Rescuer" but the industry he birthed all became "Archaeological Racist" and now they either ignore or demonize their founding father! Chances are you have never come across the photograph below.

This man's name is Heinrich Schliemann. You, Me, Archaeologists, Historians, Anthropologist, Cultural Geography, Cultural Studies, Antiquities, Historiography, Comparative Literature, Etymologists and almost 50 other educational and scientific fields of study, owe this man – A GERMAN GROCER - a thank you and a place of honor in history (but that would take supporting facts and truth and not academic oriented half-truths. Again, another whole different story).

Unfortunately the ones (Archaeologists) who should really honor Heinrich Schliemann, those who have their many accredited degrees to thank him for, actually detest and debase the man. A great man, who did great things and did mankind, academics, history and education a great favor. What was that favor he did?

> *Heinrich Schliemann believed that history as we knew it and were told was WRONG and he used his own funds to go out to find and prove TRUE HISTORY and the actual ARTIFACTS TO PROVE IT.*

Is that a "History Hunter" OR "History Looter" or "Artifact Rescuer" REVILED BY "Archaeological Racists"? You decide. To me the answer is obvious, but here is the shortened version for you to file away in your brain and use when you come up against the very same critics and criticism.

Heinrich's Wiki Background: Schliemann was born in Neubukow, Mecklenburg-Schwerin in 1822. His father, Ernst Schliemann, was a Protestant minister. The family moved to Ankershagen in 1823 (today in their house is the museum of Heinrich Schliemann). Heinrich's mother, Luise Therese Sophie, died in 1831, when Heinrich was nine years old.

After his mother's death his father sent Heinrich to live with his uncle. When he was eleven years old his father paid for him to enroll in the Gymnasium (grammar school) at Neustrelitz. Heinrich's later interest in history was initially encouraged by his father who had schooled him in the tales of the Iliad and the Odyssey and had given him a copy of Ludwig Jerrer's Illustrated History of the World for Christmas in 1829. Thus, his passion for Homer was born.

Schliemann at the age of 8, declared he would one day find and prove the city of Troy really existed!

However, Heinrich had to transfer to the Realschule (vocational school), since his family could not afford private schooling. His family's poverty made a university education impossible, so it was Schliemann's early academic experiences that influenced the course of his education as an adult. In later years, the industry he spawned and the actual academic degrees which were created as a direct result of his work and techniques  (Archaeologist); would shun his historic legacy as the industry's creator because he himself did not have a University degree.

At age 14, after leaving Realschule, Heinrich became an apprentice at Herr Holtz's grocery in Fürstenberg. He labored for five years until he was forced to leave because he burst a blood vessel lifting a heavy barrel. In 1841, Schliemann moved to Hamburg and became a cabin boy on the Dorothea, a steamer bound for Venezuela. After twelve days at sea, the ship foundered in a gale. The survivors washed up on the shores of the Netherlands. Schliemann became a messenger, office attendant, and later, a bookkeeper in Amsterdam.

On March 1, 1844, 22-year old Schliemann took a position with B. H. Schröder & Co., an import/export firm. In 1846 the firm sent him as a General Agent to St. Petersburg. In time, Schliemann represented a number of companies. He learned Russian and Greek, employing a system that he used his entire life to learn languages—Schliemann's skills allowed him to learn a new language within six weeks and wrote his diary in the language of whatever country he happened to be in.

By the end of his life, Schliemann could converse in English, French, Dutch, Spanish, Portuguese, Swedish, Polish, Italian, Greek, Latin, Russian, Arabic, and Turkish as well as German, unlike most academics at the time who only spoke Queen's English and shunned other languages. Schliemann's ability with languages was an important part of his career as a businessman in the importing trade.

In 1850, Heinrich learned of the death of his brother, Ludwig, who had become wealthy as a speculator in the California gold fields. Schliemann went to California in early 1851 and started a bank in Sacramento buying and reselling over a million dollars of gold dust in just six months. While he was there, California became the 31st state in September 1850 and Schliemann acquired United States citizenship. On April 7, 1852, he sold his business and returned to Russia. There he lived the life of a gentleman and met Ekaterina Lyschin, the niece of one of his wealthy friends.

Heinrich and Ekaterina married on October 12, 1852. Schliemann then cornered the market in indigo dye and went into the indigo business itself, turning a good profit. Ekaterina and Heinrich had a son, Sergey, and two daughters, Natalya and Nadezhda, born in 1855, 1858 and 1861 respectively. Schliemann, an entrepreneur at heart, made yet another fortune as a military contractor in the Crimean War, 1854-1856. He cornered the market in saltpeter, sulfur, and lead, constituents of ammunition, which he resold to the Russian government.

By 1858, Schliemann was wealthy enough to retire and decided to dedicate himself to the pursuit of Troy.

CHAPTER THREE

THE PRIVATELY FUNDED TREASURE HUNT THAT STARTED IT ALL!

The photo above is called the "Mask of Agamemnon" and it is one of the most well-known and recognized photos of treasure ever published. Look at that amazing artifact that was RESCUED from obscurity by someone who had the passion, funds and took the time to research and find it! A person not classically trained who wanted to prove up history, correct historical wrongs and bring precious artifacts to LIFE which were potentially buried in the earth for millennia! Sounds a lot like you and the people you metal detect, treasure hunt and ghost town explore with, doesn't it? Real people with real passions going the extra mile.

Back to Schliemann's story as recorded by Wiki:

Schliemann's first interest of a classical nature seems to have been the location of Troy.

At the time Schliemann began excavating in Turkey, the site commonly believed to be Troy was at Pınarbaşı, a hilltop at the south end of the Trojan Plain. In 1868, Schliemann visited sites in the Greek world, published Ithaka, der Peloponnesus und Troja in which he asserted that Hissarlik was the site of Troy, and submitted a dissertation in Ancient Greek proposing the same thesis to the University of Rostock. In 1869, he was awarded a PhD from the University of Rostock for that submission.

The 'Mask of Agamemnon', discovered by Heinrich Schliemann in 1876 at Mycenae now exhibited at the National Archaeological Museum of Athens.

By this time divorced from his wife and working exclusively abroad, Schliemann needed an assistant who was knowledgeable in matters pertaining to Greek culture. A friend, the Archbishop of Athens, suggested a relative of his, Sophia Engastromenos (1852–1932). They married in October 1869. They later had two children, Andromache and Agamemnon Schliemann

Schliemann began work on Troy in 1871. His excavations began before archaeology was even called archaeology and could even be considered something valuable enough for academic accreditation and study. As a direct result of Schliemann's work and success, archaeology developed into a professional field.

A cache of gold and other objects appeared in May 1873; Schliemann named it "Priam's Treasure". He later wrote that he had seen the gold glinting in the dirt and dismissed the workmen so that he and Sophia could excavate it themselves, removing it in her shawl. Sophia later wore "the Jewels of Helen" for the public. Those jewels, taken from the Pergamon Museum in Berlin by the Soviet Army (Red Army) in 1945, are now in the Pushkin Museum in Moscow.

Schliemann published his findings in 1874, in Trojanische Altertümer ("Trojan Antiquities").

This publicity backfired when the Turkish government revoked Schliemann's permission to dig and sued him for a share of the gold. Schliemann smuggled the treasure out of Turkey. He defended his "moving of the artifacts out of Turkey" as an attempt to protect the items from corrupt local officials.

Schliemann published Troja und seine Ruinen (Troy and Its Ruins) in 1875 and excavated the Treasury of Minyas at Orchomenus. In 1876, he began digging at Mycenae. Upon discovering the Shaft Graves, with their skeletons and more regal gold (including the Mask of Agamemnon), Schliemann cabled the king of Greece. The results were published in Mykenai in 1878.

Although he had received permission in 1876 to continue excavation, Schliemann did not reopen the dig site at Troy until 1878–1879, after another excavation in Ithaca designed to locate an actual site mentioned in the Odyssey. On August 1, 1890, Schliemann returned reluctantly to Athens, and in November travelled to Halle, where a long persistent chronic ear infection was operated upon. On November 13, the doctors deemed the operation a success, but his inner ear became painfully inflamed. Ignoring his doctors' advice, he left the hospital and travelled to Leipzig, Berlin, and Paris. From the latter, he planned to return to Athens in time for Christmas, but his ear condition became even worse. Too sick to make the boat ride from Naples to Greece, Schliemann remained in Naples, but managed to make a journey to the ruins of Pompeii. On Christmas Day he collapsed into a coma and died in a Naples hotel room on December 26, 1890.

The cause of death was cholesteatoma. His corpse was then transported by friends to the First Cemetery in Athens. It was interred in a mausoleum shaped like a temple erected in ancient Greek style designed by Ernst Ziller in the form of a pedimental sculpture. The frieze circling the outside of the mausoleum shows Schliemann conducting the excavations at Mycenae and other sites. His magnificent residence in the city center of Athens, houses today the Numismatic Museum of AthensNow that you have the background story of the man who actually discovered the discipline of Archaeology, here is what the Archaeological industry now projects to the world about their founding father- Heinrich Schliemann:

(1) In 1972, Professor William Calder of the University of Colorado, speaking at a commemoration of Schliemann's birthday, claimed that he had *uncovered several possible problems in Schliemann's work*. Other investigators followed, such as Professor David Traill of the University of California.

(2) An article published by the National Geographic Society called into question Schliemann's qualifications, his motives, and his methods.

(3) *"In northwestern Turkey, Heinrich Schliemann excavated the site believed to be Troy in 1870. Schliemann was a German adventurer and con man who took sole credit for the discovery, even though he was digging at the site, called Hisarlik, at the behest of British archaeologist Frank Calvert. ... Eager to find the legendary treasures of Troy, Schliemann blasted his way down to the second city, where he found what he believed were the jewels that once belonged to Helen. As it turns out, the jewels were a thousand years older than the time described in Homer's epic".*

(NOTE: There was NO SUCH accreditation as Archaeologist, yet the above calls Frank Calvert -who was doing the same as Schliemann, but was not successful- an Archaeologist. Why? Calvert was English and considered a Gentlemen – and he did not have a degree either, yet he is called an Archaeologist and Schliemann is called an "uneducated con-man". <u>This type of attempt at discrediting is still deployed today against anyone not an Archaeologist and considered a "Treasure Hunter" - Welcome to the world of Archeological and Academic Racism!</u> Another article presented similar criticisms when reporting on a speech by University of Pennsylvania scholar C. Brian Rose:

(4) *"German archaeologist Heinrich Schliemann was the first to explore the Mound of Troy in the 1870s. Unfortunately, he had had no formal education in archaeology, and dug an enormous trench "which we still call the Schliemann Trench," according to Rose, because in the process Schliemann "destroyed a phenomenal amount of material." "Only much later in his career would he accept the fact that the treasure had been found at a layer one thousand years removed from the battle between the Greeks and Trojans, and thus that it could not have been the treasure of King Priam. Schliemann may not have discovered the truth, but the publicity stunt worked, making Schliemann and the site famous and igniting the field of Homeric studies in the late 19th century".*

Talk about spitting in the face and on the history of the individual who personally, with his own funds, developed and launched the industry of Archaeology. No matter how it is put, to undertake searching and digging – private or professional – they require funding. In Schliemann's day the adventure was a sport of wealthy individuals looking for history, fame and fortune.

Here is an interesting fact: You've heard of King Tut right? It's founder, Howard Carter? Here is what Wiki and many sites say about Carter- *"Howard Carter (9 May 1874 – 2 March 1939) was an English archaeologist and Egyptologist who became world famous after discovering the intact tomb of 14th-century BC pharaoh Tutankhamun (colloquially known as "King Tut" and "the boy king")"*

Interesting fact: Carter went to Egypt at the age of 17, had no University education, but was able to go to Egypt because of family ties and being English and what do we "see" in the academic record? Carter is called both an Archaeologist and Egyptologist. See the trend? If you are "in" the right circles and from the right breeding, history will apply an advanced degree upon you and refer to you as "the degreed"; but be from nothing- an entrepreneur and out to prove history and academics wrong – you are branded a con-man, scammer or scoundrel. These are the facts, when presented to the archaeological community which enrage modern day archaeologists when used to defend treasure hunting and history hunting.

However, in an ironic turn of events, the British finally came full circle and were reborn better (remember the Ouroboros?). The Ouroboros I shared with you earlier - means to be reborn and what has happened is the country that held itself above all other people and races – especially in education and academic circles; has now become enlightened and figured out a system where both the private hunters and the archaeological accredited can co-exist and work well together.

Here is how it works in the United Kingdom (it is a great blue print):

1. All citizens can metal detect and treasure hunt and it is encouraged!

2. Why is it encouraged? There are more citizens than academics. Simple math.

3. Citizen makes a find

4. Citizen reports the find to the local Coroner (yes like the crime scene guys that pronounce the dead and cart away the dead bodies)

5. Coroner notifies the Crown

6. Crown funds the dig and restoration and AS SUCH they employ Archaeologist, Historians, Anthropologists and all kinds of academics.

7. Crown cleans up and restores the finds

8. Crown get three professional appraisals of the value of the find

9. Crown takes the appraisals average and determines value – let's say $2,000,000.

10. Crown pays the $2,000,000 to the finder and /or landowner (they split the funds)

11. Crowns thanks the finder profusely and even writes stories about them an makes them mini-celebrities

12. Crown keeps the find and puts them on public display in Museum

Did you catch that? Everyone one wins! This is the perfect win/win.

But what do American academics do? The SAME that third world countries do! Make it a crime and put people in prison – if they can. Now it is understandable why third world countries and dictators do this. They are greedy, want to sell off the treasure and pocket the funds and continue to steal from the people. But why does the United States of America do this?

The simple fact is because two issues collide.

One: Academics gets tenure and bigger University paychecks **IF** they get published and make great finds! But there is a problem.

Two: Universities no longer pay for exploration. Seems to of died in the fictional character "Indiana Jones" time period (how ironic).

Here is the conundrum: How can an Academic Archaeologist get raises, professional praise and accolades IF they institution they work for does not even pay for exploration?

It's simple, they help write laws that keep regular Joe's and Joann's from metal detecting and treasure hunting. Why? They cannot let the individual make finds because it does not benefit "me-the academic" and thus "I don't get tenure or accolades". So here is what they want.

One: You find it (although you are not supposed to)

Two: You tell them exactly where it is and give them proof of it

Three: Then "they" get you banned from the site and threaten to get you imprisoned

Four: If you have not told them the location, they try to coerce you into it so you want to save your "ass" from legal troubles

Five: They (the archaeologists and academics) then go to the site and IF something is really there, they get state and academic funds (why now? Because YOU proved it was there) and they start digging

Six: They don't get the "money from the find" so what they do (under the guise it take a lot of time) they extract fees, salaries and cost dragging out the excavation out for years and or decades (job security)

Seven: Once finished they write a book, get huge press, awards and accolades and THEY are "the discoverer" of the "find". Your name is never mentioned. I know, and they call YOU the one STEALING AND LOOTING. It's not the Seven Deadly Sins – it's the Seven Ways One Can Steal Finds Legally!

Yep, our U.S. system is messed up, but one day the system might become enlightened and embracing and learn that there are millions of people who will scour every inch of land in the US, if the system who not threaten them, would give them credit and incentive and then the **TWO DIFFERENT SYSTEMS** become partners. Now that works and the British proved it.

Happy Hunting and as always know the laws and rules and have a grand adventure!

BUT, before we get to the 10 Treasure Legends, I am going to do a little bit of a refresher from some of my earlier writings so you can understand both the nature of Treasure Legends and the facts and fictions that always surround them.

So, just a little refresher course, because with at least a little bit of understanding of how to find treasure, then maybe the reading experience will be that much better for you.

CHAPTER FOUR

MILLIONS, BILLIONS, OR TRILLIONS?

Billions of dollars in lost treasure waiting to be found? That figure must seem outrageous, or at the very least incorrect? If you wondered this to yourself, then you are actually right. There are not billions of dollars out there in lost treasures waiting to be reclaimed. There are trillions of dollars of treasure waiting to be reclaimed. But, I was faced with making a choice when it came to publishing this book. Would I be able to convince the public at large there were millions or even billions to recover, much less trillions? I chose the middle road, a number far more conservative than any realistic assessment. Why?

Most people, right off the top of their heads, could **NOT** tell you how many zeros are in one trillion.

Well, one trillion is 1,000,000,000,000. **1 2 3 4 5 6 7 8 9 10 11 12** - that's **twelve** zeroes.

In fact, to give you a better perspective, in the state of Texas alone, where I am sitting as I write this, there is an estimated $99,581,605,263 (ninety-nine billion) in documented unrecovered lost treasures. Compare that to Florida at $201,608,423,684 (two hundred and one billion) or New Mexico at $365,684,242,105 (three hundred and sixty-five billion) and you can easily see how the numbers rack up. But this is still not quite correct.

The numbers for this book were figured using the daily average price of gold on a day over four months ago. Now, as of this writing, gold is up an additional 32%; this means that Texas treasure is worth $31,866,113,684.16 (thirty-one billion) more, while Florida's treasure is worth an extra $64,514,695,578.88 (sixty-four billion) and New Mexico's an extra $117,018,957,473.60 (one hundred seventeen billion).

Absolutely boggles the mind, does it not? You will learn more about these numbers and where they come from in this book. But first and foremost, this book is not about the values of lost treasures now or in the past, but rather the passion and lore that goes into treasure hunting. If you understand history and treasure and the nature of both, you are moving along the road toward becoming a real treasure hunter. Men have sought out the lost, hidden, stored, and cached treasures of others from the beginning of time. Treasure hunting is thousands of years older than the profession of archaeology, and in fact it is the pursuit of treasure that birthed the profession of archaeology.

There are many forms of treasure seekers, from those who seek documents to those who seek artifacts and mineral sources, since treasure itself comes in many forms. In fact, there are papers and books that have been lost to time which are now as valuable as a ton of gold!

There are many different levels of seekers as well. There are the treasure seekers who do it for recreation, those who do it for adventure, and those who do it to shore up historical research. The rarest of the treasure seekers are those who make up the professional class of treasure hunters: those who shun the name treasure hunter, due to the modern implications of that label, and who have gone to the trouble of both the education and certification to become what is professionally called **Cacheologists**.

Cacheology:

The profession whereby highly trained and certified individuals, using archaeological methods combined with forensic historical research and modern technology, set out to prove or disprove, dispel or recover, set the historical record straight or professionally document, the various types of caches, common treasures or otherwise, that have been lost to history and mankind. The mission of the Cacheologists is to use profit-driven methods to recover lost caches for the expansion of mankind's study, education, instruction, collection, showcasing, and preservation. Cacheology is the professional rescue and preservation of caches that time and the environment would otherwise rapidly and thoroughly destroy, erasing historical records and artifacts vital and irreplaceable for the entire world.

CHAPTER FIVE

CACHEOLOGY

Any Treasure is in fact a cache. A cache is some form of valuables that has been stored, either willingly or under duress, but which was never retrieved. There various forms of caches as well. They are as follows:

1. Cache of *Ceremony*
2. Cache of *Convenience*
3. Cache of *Catastrophe*
4. Cache of *Duress*
5. Cache of *Criminal Activity*
6. Cache of *Nature*

If you understand the nature of a cache, or in other words, if you understand how the cache originally became a cache, you then have a better chance of verifying, locating, and recovering the cache. Below I will give you the formal Cacheological definition of each of these different types of caches, but as you read this book, bear in mind that if you can learn to identify the type of a particular cache, you may have what it takes to become a professional treasure hunter.

CACHE OF CEREMONY

A Cache of Ceremony is the style of cache that has been deposited where it was found (or is yet to be found) due to the nature of the culture and ceremonies that generated the cache to begin with. For example, the treasure of King Tut is exactly this type of cache. Ancient Egyptians buried their dead kings with all of their treasures. Their culture, ceremonies, and religious protocols demanded such; thus, the treasure of King Tut is a Cache of Ceremony. So the rule of thumb for a cache identified as a Cache of Ceremony is: If it was the cultural norm for priests, rulers, and/or notables to be buried in a specific religious or ceremonial style and location, then when you find those you will find the cache. Understand and re-create the ceremony and you can locate the cache.

CACHE OF CONVENIENCE

Convenience is exactly that, where it was convenient to store the cache. These caches were not moved from place to place; they were just stored for convenience. It is also the type of cache utilized by workers, common men, and lay people. Why? There are no ceremonies or cultural standards involved in dictating where to stash the cache. For example, it is said there was more money cached away during the Great Depression than there was stored in banks, and billions and billions of that is still cached in the same hiding places. During the Great Depression, people did not trust banks, so they stored their money, valuables and gold in places only known to them, but surely convenient to them. Those places would be in fencepost holes, water wells, fireplaces, floorboards, and such. Another Cache of Convenience, which actually goes hand in hand with a Cache of Catastrophe (defined below), is anywhere a large battle took place. How? Think of the thousands and thousands of soldiers and warriors in time past that would go to war. Along with them they carried their pay (they could not transfer funds to banks back and forth like we did) and their rings, body ornaments, metals, and religious statuaries. Most of these were various forms of precious metals. Before battle, but near the troops actual staging area or camp, each soldier would conveniently (there is that word again) bury his or her personal belongings and fortunes before going into battle. This way they were assured not to lose them and their personal caches would not fall into the hands of the enemy.

Now consider just how many of the warriors would not come back from the battle. Of course, these caches were put there by the attacking army, not any city which was attacked by surprise. So, especially due to invading Roman armies, there are hundreds of thousands, if not millions, of personal soldier or warrior caches in and around camps, staging areas and battlegrounds. 10,000 dead warriors add up to tons of recovered cache troves in each battle area.

CACHE OF CATASTROPHE

Catastrophe is a harsh word. A harsh word for harsh circumstances. Disaster, war, earthquake, shipwreck: chose any word that means that people and their places and/or modes of transport are destroyed, then you understand the concept of Cache of Catastrophe.

Spanish and Chinese treasure ships going down in hurricanes are Caches of Catastrophe. Where the catastrophe happened is where the cache was deposited. An ancient temple or library destroyed by a massive earthquake and dropped off into the sea to never be seen again is a Cache of Catastrophe, and where the catastrophe happened, the cache lays in wait for the Cacheologist.

Understand the nature and scope of the catastrophe and you can locate the cache, but remember, by its very nature a Cache of Catastrophe is either at the bottom of the ocean or buried under tons and tons of ancient debris covered in turn by the debris and buildup of time. These caches may be fairly easy to locate but very hard and expensive to recover.

CACHE OF DURESS

Logically you might question, "What is really the difference between duress and catastrophe?" The simple answer is **SURVIVAL**. Yes, an unexpected attack of an army or Indians is a catastrophe, and those things and people caught up in the catastrophe ultimately lay exactly where the catastrophe happened. But what about the survivors? There are almost always survivors; how else would we know the historical facts, places, people, and issues, except from those that survived. Indian attacks, routed armies, and flight from pursuers are all causes of caches of duress.

Now put yourself in the survivors' situation. All hell is breaking loose. You grab your family and valuables and haul ass. Literally. The survivor is running away from the catastrophe and invariably the transport of their valuables become too much and they hurriedly bury or conceal their cache to be retrieved later. The outlaws with the posse on their tail does not get the gold or bankroll back to their lair or hideout, they have pursuers right behind them, and they hurriedly bury or stash the cache. They don't have the time or luxury to hide the cache very deep or with much sophistication, or to make sure it's not detectable if someone were to come across it.

So, due to the fact that Caches of Duress are survivors or those on the run from imminent danger, the caches they hide are done hurriedly and on the run, and therefore are not deep or very well hidden. These may be the easiest caches to recover, but due to the nature of the situation, they can be spread over a very large area and may in fact be smaller, though not necessarily less valuable. Find the paths taken by those fleeing and along the way you may find many a cache.

CACHE OF CRIMINAL ACTIVITY

Criminals have patterns, partners, and hide outs. Understand those and you understand where to find Caches of Criminal Activity. Yes, in Caches of Duress, I spoke of bandits on the run, so were they not criminals as well, and shouldn't they be listed here? Yes and no. The key is full understanding of the nature of the cache. Yes, the bandit was a criminal, but in that instance, thus the nature of the cache you are seeking, the criminal was on the run being pursued. Therefore they did not reach their hideout, partners in crime, or territory, and they were forced to act under duress.

Remember, understand the nature of the cache and you can find where it is. If you are searching for a trove of gold stolen by Jesse James, and you know that he stole it, fled, and was apprehended (only to escape later), but no gold was found with him, the facts tell you — no, scream to you — that it was stashed on the run. So, do not waste your time looking at his family home or favorite hideout for that particular treasure. But look into the gangsters, bandits, criminals, and drug lords who got away with their ill-gotten goods, and chances are the cache is hidden within their associated network of lairs, hideouts, properties, and partners' properties.

Criminals are notorious for protecting their hidden hoards, and in order to do so the criminal must be within eyeshot, hearing, or quick response distance from the cache. Thus, know the nature of the cache and you can find the cache.

CACHE OF NATURE

Gold, platinum, diamonds, sapphires, and such, do not necessarily have to be mined, minted, and shaped into a royal crown to be considered treasure. Nature is the single largest hider and hoarder of caches. Mother Nature is the single richest individual in the world. Bill Gates and Warren Buffet don't even come a close second to her. Mother Nature is so loaded with treasure she can afford to deposit a trillion dollars in gold or diamonds in a single location and never go back to retrieve them, much less expose them, for millions of years. Most treasure hunters forget this source of wealth, but the professional, the Cacheologist is trained to find these caches as well. In fact, to the Cacheologists, this form of cache is considered low-hanging fruit and ends up being the source of funding for their formal cache expeditions.

Millions upon millions of Caches of Nature exist and someone, somewhere in history has stumbled across them and left us a record and facts to follow. The only thing that happened is the original discoverer of the cache could not remember or relocate the exact location of the cache and therefore could never retrieve it. The easiest example of this is the tons of legends and historical facts surrounding lost gold mines. At some point in time, a prospector came across one of Mother Nature's cache hiding places, but by not paying close attention to their surrounding landmarks or through other circumstances, the prospector went into the nearest town to file their claim, get help, or get supplies and tools and could not find their way back to the natural cache site. There is no way to really put a value on these types of caches because one single cache of nature could be worth a trillion dollars in today's precious metals market, and there are literally thousands upon thousands of these found but lost again Caches of Nature.

But following the clues Mother Nature leaves and stories in the historical record of finds, one could find billions in a single location. If you don't believe me, just ask our Canadian friend and diamond expert, Mr. Fripke. Understand the nature of the cache and you can find the cache.

CHAPTER SIX

FILL IN THE BLANKS AND FIND YOUR FORTUNE!

One of most common questions someone asks when they find out you are a Professional Treasure Hunter or Cacheologist, is: "What does it take to be able to find lost treasure?" For me the answer is always the same. Even though we use some sophisticated equipment, venture into dangerous environments and brave terrains and situations most people would never venture into, the **KEY** to successful treasure hunting and recovery is (and in my mind will always be) **GREAT RESEARCH**.

GREAT RESREARCH, that's it. Great research is over 90% of the successful treasure hunting process. No special equipment or special physical prowess will ever replace good old fashioned research. Now, for the first time in the history of humanity, we have more research tools and abilities at our fingertips. Yes, sometimes you do have to travel to an area and go to the local records or tax office to find the information you seek, but now most of what you need to research is only as far as your computer.

Think of a computer or your home computer as the most valuable treasure hunting tool you have. My Grandmother died at the age of 103. I would have many conversations with her about history and technology. These conversations gave me a very unique perspective on just how much the world has changed. She marveled at automobiles, air travel and even lived to see fax machines and computers. She was impressed with just how far mankind had come during her day. Now, I think to my days as a child. The use of computers in schools only came to be prevalent once I was leaving high school. Video games to play on your TV came a few years later and then a decade later here come fax machines, and I was amazed when I could call a records office and they could fax me the information the same day and not have to be the standard records request by mail and then wait a couple of weeks to get a response and hard copy in the mail. Then along come bulletin boards, email and eventually the Internet.

Those of you closely familiar with my background know I literally have hundreds of Internet patents and Technology patents, so needless to say, I know the power of technology. When I became in tune and familiar with the Internet and what it would eventually become, I knew it would change the world as we knew it. Back then, I was excited about just being able to see text on a computer screen that someone else wrote. In fact, when I first become involved in technology, there were **NO** pictures on the Internet, no web browsers, no music and it was a rip roaring speed of 2800 baud (for you of those who don't know, compared to today's broadband, G4 or G5 and other new technologies) that was the blinding speed equivalent of my 103 year old grandmother trying to outrun a fighter jet. There just is no comparison – at all!

Today we literally have the world of information at our fingertips and even powerful countries such as China, Korea, Iraq and Iran cannot keep outside information away from the common populace. The Internet is too big, too free and too powerful to contain or control. No more Dark Ages, where the Church tells you what to think or say. No more learning only the government approved or ruling party version of a story or subject. It is now all wide open for anyone who wants to know. Even the modern news business, TV and print media alike, are almost and I stress **ALMOST** no longer able to contain or spin stories to their own will and sensationalism. Now, with the advent of the Internet, we are getting closer to a revolution of Pure Truth.

I truly believe and stress to my children, now is an amazing time to live in. No, we are not making mad dashes of exploration to jungles or the Poles, as was recent centuries past, but we are now poised to both **REWRITE** and **CORRECT** history and get the message to the entire world. All of this is directly a result of technology being put in the hands of everyone!

So how does this relate to Treasure Hunting? Not too long ago, someone wanting to do research into a long lost treasure would have to visit libraries (several of them since different libraries would carry different books and reference libraries), travel to tax and records offices and send tons of letters requesting information and hope, just hope you got a response, that sometimes only came a month or even, many months later if you were lucky.

Now – as an absolute truth, "Ask and You Shall Receive", all thanks to the Internet.

Since research is 90% of the success of a treasure hunt, and now you have books, public records, military records and every book ever published at your fingertips, you are a master at research and thus can be a master at Treasure Research, and thus Treasure Hunting.

It **IS** as simple as **"FILL IN THE BLANKS AND FIND YOUR FORTUNE"**.

This book series is all about the research process. In this state by state book series is treasure of every single type. Hidden Hoards, Caches, Stolen Loot, Lost Mines and Forgotten Fortunes, they are all in between these covers. Whether your favorite type of treasure is in Ghost Towns, buried vaults, in desert sands, in mountain hideaways or at the bottom of the seas, there is treasure here for you to find. All you have to do is fill in the blanks.

Some of the stories inside are loaded with such great facts and clues that all someone has to do is load up in their car, get out at the location with a shovel and dig. Other stories in this book will take research work, some more than others and even better, some of the stories in my various books are **TOTAL** misdirection (only four of them in all my books so don't worry about them being too many of them). Why would

I include total horse hockey in any of my books? So you can learn to tell the difference, as the saying goes, "between poop and shoe polish." Kind of hard I know, I am that way. Why would anyone, truly interested in finding lost treasure want fluff and puff? Fluff and Puff is for certain kinds of movies and has no business in the profession of, or for that matter, the recreation of; treasure hunting. Only the hard core facts will pay out.

But you do need to be able to tell the difference between writers' story telling gunk and good, provable treasure clues and leads. So, this book has a little of everything allowing you to hone your skills and hopefully make a fortune.

In my passion of research, my formal team research, and in my schools I use a simple rule called 3x3x3 **C.A.C.H.E.** system. The acronym of **C.A.C.H.E.** is the actual formula for being wildly successful at cache hunting and recovery.

> **C – Consolidate**
>
> **A – Authenticate/audit**
>
> **C – Cull**
>
> **H – History/historical records**
>
> **E – Explore/expedition**

C.A.C.H.E is the key to cache. If you take the time to fully understand and employ the steps of the cache acronym, then you could become very successful and very wealthy. It all begins and ends with you and your efforts.

C IS FOR CONSOLIDATE

Invariably there are many different versions of any given treasure story. It's the old "telephone game" most of us played as children. Put a classroom of kids in the circle. Whisper a simple to remember phrase or story into the ear of the first student and then have them pass it on in secret to the next student; and so on and so on.

By the time the story comes around back to the teacher, the phrase only minimally resembles the original phrase given to the first student. There four reasons for this phenomenon.

1. **Poor listening skills**
2. **Poor translation skills**
3. **Willful maliciousness**
4. **Human nature**

If you grasp why stories change from person to person and can decipher where they went astray, then you are rapidly and intelligently headed down the path to cache recovery success. It is easy to understand poor listening skills. Most people do not really listen to the actual details of a story. Hundreds and thousands of years ago, when stories were only communicated by word of mouth, people tended to get the story accurate and retell it as told to them. It was a source of pride and was an absolute requirement of the storyteller to get facts flawless. In fact, being the culture's or area's storyteller was a true and noble profession.

However, the advent of published works and with the changes in modern society, we have moved storytelling from truth and accurateness to sensationalism, errors, omissions, and bending the truth to suit one's needs.

Poor translation skills not only mean being unable to retell the story as originally told, it also relates to the literal mistranslation of words between cultures and races of people. Such as the common mistranslation of the meaning of the word "church" as it applies to the Bible. For example:

The English word "church" has various meanings. Webster gives the following definitions for the word church.

1.   a building for public Christian worship.
2.   a religious service in such a building.
3.   (sometimes cap.)
     A.   *the world body of Christian believers; Christendom.*
     B.*any major division of his body; a Christian denomination.*
4.   a Christian congregation.
5.   organized religion as distinguished from the state.
6.   (cap)
     A.   *The Christian church before the Reformation.*
     B.*the Roman Catholic Church.*
7.   the profession of an ecclesiastic -V. C.
8.   to perform a church service of thanksgiving for (a woman after child birth). [Go RI (a)on (DOA) the Lord's house).

Today the word church has a wide variety of meanings from referring to a building to performing a religion service. Although we have an understanding the modern use of the word, it is of more significance in understanding the use of the word in the New Testament. It is essential that we understand its original meaning as it was used in New Testament times.

In our English Bible the Greek word, "ekklesia" is translated in most places "church." The word "ekklesia" is found in one hundred and fifteen places in the New Testament. It is translated in English one hundred and thirteen times "church" and the remaining times it is translated "assembly." In classical Greek the word "ekklesia" meant "an assembly of citizens summoned by the crier, the legislative assembly." The word as used in the New Testament is taken from the root of this word, which simply means to "call out." In New Testament times the word was exclusively used to represent a group of people assembled together for a particular cause or purpose. It was never used exclusively to refer to a "religious meeting or group on a building"

An examination of the Greek word "ekklesia" reveals that the word is properly translated into English as the "assembly" or "congregation." It is used to refer to a group of persons that are organized together for a common purpose and who meet together, and was used as early as the 5th Century B.C.

So the word as originally written, shared, and spoken meant one thing, and today we have other completely different meanings. Case in point: there was a time your gay friends meant those who were "happy," not those in "same sex" relationships. So understanding that poor translations skills always come into play is part of the **C.A.C.H.E.** equation.

Now here comes the can of worms, willful maliciousness, and funny how it follows my comments on the church, since one of the most egregious offenders of this in historical terms and culture terms is the institution of the Church. Throughout history (there is that word again history) stories have been modified, augmented, and embellished to reflect favorably on the ruling class, which in most cases was the Church. Now, remember earlier when I mentioned that there is a practice among treasure lore and lost mine writers to willfully omit facts, leads, elements of case and point to hide the actual facts that made lead to a caches discovery? Well, this is most common fact of interference of man when it comes to cache history and lore. Most of the stories get willingly perverted and the truth compromised.

This point, now naturally leads us to the nature of Mankind. Man, whether in his DNA or his soul tends to embellish for various reasons, i.e. **(a)** deception, **(b)** personal gain, **(c)** entertainment, **(d)** self-preservation, or; **(e)** self-importance or ego. Let's face it. Most people love attention, love being the center of attention, the topic of the story, and the ironically enough, the bearer of bad news.

Bearer of bad news? Who likes to be the bearer of bad news? Well, think about it. All adventurers and explores are commonly sent off by people who relish telling them **(1)** they are fools, **(2)** chasing a dream,

(3) wasting their lives, (4) will die in the process, and (5) will find nothing! Read any account of famous expeditions. This is just a fact of life and the nature of mankind. Most want to be "The Winners" but do not want others "to," win." You have those people in your life right now and I bet you can easily identify them – the dream killers, the moaners and the "you-can't-do-that" crowd. If you have trouble identifying them in your life, announce you are going on a treasure hunt and stand back and watch their individual responses to your announcements. You know these types of people, and they will always reveal themselves!

So how does all of this relate to **CONSOLIDATE**? The first step in mastering **C.A.C.H.E.** is to consolidate everything you can find published, written, noted, and said about the particular cache you are interested in tracking down. This may be 10 items or a thousand items, but consolidate it all in one central place where you can read, reread, research, and study over and over again. Then, with your understanding of the four historical story and legend phenomena, i.e.

1. **Poor listening skills**
2. **Poor translation skills**
3. **Willful maliciousness**
4. **Human nature**

Start shifting through your information so you can get to the **A** in the **C.A.C.H.E.** formula.

A IS FOR AUTHENTICATE

Authenticate, as defined by the Merriam-Webster Dictionary is a transitive verb: to prove or serve to prove the authenticity of (authenticate a document).

This is the most important step up to this point. Of all the materials, documents, stories, versions of stories, magazine articles, newspaper clippings, and/or firsthand accounts; you must take steps to determine which of them are authentic. For me, I sometimes make a personal columned grid where I lay out the common threads between each of the versions of the story told. When you lay out the details in a grid and look at them as various points of facts, and they are not crowded and drowned in a sea of letters and words, but presented as bullet points, you can start to recognize patterns. This is one of the very same steps a forensic researcher or F. B. I. profiler starts to create a "description or identity" of a serial killer. The various facts, when arranged properly, can reveal clues; important clues that can be easily overlooked.

But at the very same time you are revealing hidden clues, you are also discriminating fact from fiction. You will be able to identify fancy story telling from factual events that will actually lead to the recovery of the cache. Also during this process you are able to identify the subtle changes over time, writer after writer, story teller after story teller; and be able to discern whether something has been either repeated as true or omitted for one reason or another. If you arrange your **CONSOLIDATION** work and sort them during your **AUTHENTICATION** process chronologically, then you are afforded one more edge: history (which will play a huge role later on as you will read). Comparing stories told or retold by chronological dates, allows you to work your way back to the original source; and the closer to the source the more reliable the information. Remember, detectives don't want to interview the friend of a friend who had a friend that saw the crime occur; they want to get to either the dying victims account or the first person witness accounts. And so do you when it comes to Cacheology. Why? So you can begin the next step in the process, **CULL**.

C IS FOR CULL

Here is another transitive verb from Merriam-Webster.
CULL:

1. to select from a group; choose (culled the best passages from the poet's work)
2. to reduce or control the size of (as a herd) by removal (as by hunting) of especially weaker animals; also to hunt or kill (animals) as a means of population control.

Cull, crudely put, is a means of **"CRAP"** control. You need to weigh through the fanciful fabrications and cut to the chase to glean the information that will actually allow you to find the cache. Do not waste your time with useless facts or just decide to pursue a cache hunt with only one story or very little facts. You need fact after verifiable fact. My Professional rule of thumb in going after a particular cache is: three different stories, three different geological anchors, and three verifiable historical accounts or record sources proving the three stories, sources, and individuals involved.

Yes, **3x3x3;** it's my matrix formula of verification and begins the culling process. To give you an example of each: If a particular lost mine story has a particular individual's name attached to it, then verify the existence of the individual. If they found the mine and then somewhere along the way they were killed but told no one about the mine, then there may very well exist a mining claim at the claims office. If it was a huge find of gold and the individual needed sources, tools, and funds to mine the claim, then there will more than likely be an assay record and partnership record and that can verify various points.

If the story of the fantastic claim was written about in the local paper, do a few things: (1) check the papers story against the legend, and (2) check the newspaper writers past stories on the topic. Why the second? Was the newspaper man a "fact reporter" or the papers "fanciful writer"? The first lends more credence to the story, the second means you have to find other sources and not trust this newspaperman's account.

Don't get upset or discouraged if you throw out 80% or more of your collected stories on the cache. That's normal and in fact culling more is normal. Use my proven 3x3x3 method of verifying and culling and you too could be a successful cache hunter. If you do you will make history (there is that word again).

H IS FOR HISTORY

History & Historical

Hearsay & Headaches

Hard Work & Head Work

Hysterical & Heartache

Hard fought & Happiness

Each they hunt, hand in hand

The words above have a connection. Each positive begets a positive. Conversely, each negative begets a negative. It is all in how you approach your cache mindset. History is the single most important factor in validating, pinpointing, and recovering a particular cache. If you have history on your side then it is almost as good as having a time machine that will take you back to the very moment in time the cache was deposited.

Whether or not a person means to, they do leave their stamp somewhere along the historical record: censuses, military records, property ownership, shipping manifest and passenger lists. Somewhere the information you seek exists. Searching property records, death and tax records, and information at the local library can go a long way to validating your leads and facts about a certain cache.

If you can go to historic sources and verify the story or lead, and if you can put it into historical context, i.e. three days journey in the 1800s would have been up to a **MAX** of 60 miles, whereby in more recent times, you could have traveled across the whole of the US by car in three days' time. Historical context is paramount. I learned the historical context point the hard way one time when I was looking for an old miner's cabin. I looked and looked for a log cabin but could not find one, and the only broken down wooden structure was a corral. However, the stone miner's cabin was easily found when I corrected for the historical context and location context. A simple change made all the difference in the world.

Adjust your clues according to **HISTORY** and **HISTORICAL CONTEXT** and save yourself a lot of false starts and dead ends.

Now, when reading the stories in this book, please keep in mind the **C.A.C.H.E.** method of detection and validation and see how many clues you can pick out from the stories told and then turn the stories told herein into your very own personal Treasure Case Files.

Now the

E IS FOR EXPLORE

so let's get exploring!

CHAPTER SEVEN

HOW TO BUILD YOUR PERSONAL TREASURE CASE FILES

The difference between a treasure story and a treasure case file is the case file has the relevant clues notated, researched, plotted and ready to put to work for the treasure hunter or Cacheologist.

There are certain things that make a case file a real case file. First, of course, is to stick to the 3x3x3: **<u>3 Different Sources</u>** for the same story, from 3 different geological anchors or perspectives with 3 at least three verifiable individuals who were involved in the same treasure story

Now most people ask, "What are the all elements to the 3x3x3 process?" One, there is **NO WAY** to list all the individual elements needed to verify, cross check and re-verify, but there is a starting point. Besides, as any good researcher knows, the more one investigates, the more clues are found that require further investigation. So, you start with the basics and from there the treasure verification matrix expands, up and until the point you have more than enough information to find what you are looking for, and then you have to get off your duff and go out and get it!

As you read the stories inside, you will notice the following check list or table at the end of each treasure story:

Who:_____

What:_____

Where:_____

How:_____

Others:_____

Records/Relatives:_____

Tax/Death/Military:_____

Newspapers:_____

  Internet:_____

  Sources:_____

COMMENTS:_____

_____
_____
_____
_____
_____
_____
_____

It is this checklist that will enable you to transform these stories into your very own, highly personalized, Treasure Case Files. You might find you want to go research several treasures at once or you may read this book and just select one that meets your personal criteria and likes. From there, you begin the process of making the case file and as with all good detective or forensic research work, you begin with the **WHO**, **WHAT**, **WHERE**, **WHEN** and **HOW**.

In journalism, the **Five Ws** (also known as the Five Ws (and one H), or Six Ws) is a concept in news style, research, and in police investigations that are regarded as basics in information-gathering. It is a formula for getting the "full" story on something. The maxim of the Five Ws (and one H) is that for a report to be considered complete it must answer a checklist of six questions, each of which comprises an interrogative word:

Who? *Who was involved?*

What? *What happened (what's the story)?*

Where? *Where did it take place?*

When? *When did it take place?*

Why? *Why did it happen?*

How? *How did it happen?*

These principles, as with Journalism, Detective work or any forensic research work, also apply to the research work needed to verify, authenticate and locate lost treasures. The principle underlying the maxim is that each question should elicit a factual answer, thus facts necessary to include for a report to be considered complete. Importantly, none of these questions can be answered with a simple "yes" or "no".

Simple yes or no answers, as with any forensic research, does not **VERIFY** or validate any clues for you to follow to find your treasure. You need facts and as many facts as possible. But, the **WHO, WHAT, WHERE, WHEN, WHY** and **HOW** only answer a few of the questions needed to discover the location of a lost treasure. You need to know more. You need to create a map of times, places, people and things, but most important you need to know these facts are reliable. That brings us to the other basic treasure case file questions that need to be asked. On your checklist at the end of each story we have included **OTHERS**.

OTHERS — why others? Simply put, **IF** there were **OTHERS** (additional people involved in the treasure story) then you need to answer the basic questions about all the parties or players involved. When researching one person's background you may come to dead end leads, but when you research everyone involved, it **MOST LIKELY** will give you answers about other people as well and new contacts and links to research out. Simply put, other people involved may give up more clues than the single main player. So **OTHERS** are there to remind you to fully research **ALL** involved and ask yourself "Who else?"

The next items listed are:

RECORDS - RELATIVES - TAX - DEATH - MILITARY

These are self-explanatory, but they are reminders of where to look for additional verification and validation information. Are there shipment records? Did they have relatives in the area? Surviving relatives? Death records? Ancestry Records? Did they serve in the Military? The comprehensive search of these types of records, which are available online, will help you find out more about the players and the **OTHERS** and can actually lead to more **OTHERS**. Remember, when it comes to treasure hunting, the more people involved, the more chance of finding clues and leads.

CHAPTER 7 HOW TO BUILD YOUR PERSONAL TREASURE CASE FILES

Next on your story checklist comes:

NEWSPAPERS and **WHAT**

In the beginning of this book I talked about how important using the Internet for research is, but when it comes to Newspapers and the articles and stories of the past, most are on the Internet, just not searchable by the Internet standards. That means, you can't just type in words and hope to find old newspaper stories. Most of the old newspaper stories from the 1700's and 1800's are only scanned in as images, and that means the Internet cannot search for the words in them, so when you do a basic search on the Net, you miss most of the newspaper stories. So the **NEWSPAPERS** section is here to remind you to search the areas **NEWSPAPER**. If it happened in Mesa, Arizona then search the Mesa, Arizona Newspaper via various Newspaper Archives. Once you have logged into the archive, then you can search their system remotely and find what you need. Basically as weird as it sounds it's available over the Net but not on the Net. It's on the Newspaper Archive Files.

And that leads to another **WHAT**, simply meaning **IF** you found a newspaper archive story, **WHAT did it say?** Compare it to the other information you collected.

While searching for a $10 Billion, yes, $10 Billion Dollar lost treasure, I read many books written on the topic and tons of accounts, but it was one rare, very rare newspaper article from 1946 that quoted word for

www.ExpeditionHistory.org
www.TreasureBusiness.org COPYRIGHT 2014 JHP **67**

word an article from 1810 that gave me the new and valuable information I needed to find the treasures clues.

INTERNET and **SOURCES** is there to remind you to write down and digitally store your Internet Sources for your fact finding. The Internet grows daily and servers go down and websites go out of business hourly. Don't just think you can remember the website you found the information from, chances are you cannot. The volume of information is much too great. So **LOG** your Internet sites and your sources. This means the **WHOLE** web address and not just a name of a website. Again the pages of a web site grow daily and thus pages change daily and server space is made daily by discarding old files. Those files just may be the old story you thought you could go back to.

As a rule of thumb, I do the following on Internet Based sources:

1. **ADD** the **LINK** to your Favorites file in your Web Browser
2. **PRINT** a **HARD COPY** of the information for your hard files
3. **SAVE** a **MIRROR COPY** of the websites pages containing the information you needed and store this to your hard drive. There are many software programs that can mirror image a web page for your computer.
4. **BACK UP! BACK UP! BACK UP ALL YOUR FILES!**

And finally, I have added a **COMMENTS** section so you can add comments on a treasure story as you are inspired and don't lose it by trying to remember to notate it later

READ THIS BOOK WITH A PEN IN HAND!! GO AHEAD AND GET ONE, I WILL WAIT!

And since most people need to be told three times to remember something, well so, here you are. Are you willing to fill in the blanks?

The only thing standing between you and a fortune in lost gold is **RESEARCH.**

If you are willing to fill in the blanks, you can fill your pockets with a fortune.

Got something to write with?

Then let's get going!

CHAPTER EIGHT

MISSOURI

CASS COUNTY HIDDEN TREASURE

CASS COUNTY HIDDEN TREASURE

Of all the various groups of explorers and settlers traveling through America in the 1700s, the Spanish were probably the richest. Spain had control over all of the countries in the South America and Central America regions, and they were simply exploding with wealth, in the form of jewels, diamonds, gold, silver, and valuables of every kind of gem known to man. Their massive treasures are one of the reasons that the pirates of that era loved to pinpoint a Spanish ship on the horizon; they knew they had hit the jackpot and would soon be making a fortune from their looting activities.

Other than traveling on ships back to Spain, much of the treasure was used to finance the explorers who were also in the west conducting expeditions throughout the country. They were looking for unclaimed lands and property and used gold to pay for their supplies during the trips. When they arrived at their destinations, they would have the treasures to establish a new fort or camp in the area.

One such expedition took place in 1772, but did not have the intended result. A large group of Spaniards were traveling north near the current town of Harrisonville, Missouri. Their long wagon train contained many valuables and supplies, including fifteen separate wagons of gold, each weighing one hundred and thirty pounds. Another few wagons were carrying one thousand pure silver bars. Each bar weighed twenty pounds. Calculating the total value of just the gold and silver could make one's head spin; it is a whopping thirty-four million dollars at today's prices.

When the expedition stopped to make camp, it took several hours for the workers to bury the treasure underground, just yards from the trail. They divided the gold from the silver and buried them into two separate caches. Soon after the treasures were buried, Indians came hunting on the prowl and attacked the Spanish explorers. Most of the expedition was killed and the remaining alive were scattered into the wilderness, where they died from starvation and dehydration. The Indians confiscated all of the supplies, wagons, and other valuables.

Centuries passed, and the attack was all but forgotten until a group of bridge contractors were digging in the area in 1930 and encountered ancient Spanish weapons, Indian artifacts, and a slew of skeletons. A bit of research confirmed that it was in the exact region of the Indian slaughter on the Spanish expedition.

The location of the buried treasure is believed to be located five miles west and one mile north of Harrisonville, Missouri. The silver and gold are buried one mile north and south of each other. The location is situated just twenty-five miles south of Kansas City, in a wilderness area just north of South Hope Road in Peculiar, Missouri. The separate location of the silver was said to be further east, near the southern end of South Treasure Road, near the Rodman School in Cass County.

Who:_____

What:_____

Where:_____

How:_____

Others:_____

Records/Relatives:_____

Tax/Death/Military:_____

Newspapers:_____

    Internet:_____

    Sources:_____

COMMENTS:_____

_____

_____

_____

_____

_____

_____

_____

_____

_____

Who:_____

What:_____

Where:_____

How:_____

Others:_____

Records/Relatives:_____

Tax/Death/Military:_____

Newspapers:_____

    Internet:_____

    Sources:_____

COMMENTS:_____

_____

_____

_____

_____

_____

_____

_____

_____

_____

Who:_____

What:_____

Where:_____

How:_____

Others:_____

Records/Relatives:_____

Tax/Death/Military:_____

Newspapers:_____

    Internet:_____

    Sources:_____

COMMENTS:_____

_____

_____

_____

_____

_____

_____

_____

_____

_____

Who:_____

What:_____

Where:_____

How:_____

Others:_____

Records/Relatives:_____

Tax/Death/Military:_____

Newspapers:_____

    Internet:_____

    Sources:_____

COMMENTS:_____

_____

_____

_____

_____

_____

_____

_____

_____

_____

Who:_____

What:_____

Where:_____

How:_____

Others:_____

Records/Relatives:_____

Tax/Death/Military:_____

Newspapers:_____

    Internet:_____

    Sources:_____

COMMENTS:_____

_____

_____

_____

_____

_____

_____

_____

_____

_____

_____

Who:_____

What:_____

Where:_____

How:_____

Others:_____

Records/Relatives:_____

Tax/Death/Military:_____

Newspapers:_____

Internet:_____

Sources:_____

COMMENTS:_____

_____

_____

_____

_____

_____

_____

_____

_____

_____

NOTES

_____
_____
_____
_____
_____
_____
_____
_____
_____
_____
_____
_____
_____
_____
_____
_____
_____
_____
_____
_____
_____
_____

NOTES

_____

_____

_____

_____

_____

_____

_____

_____

_____

_____

_____

_____

_____

_____

_____

_____

_____

_____

NOTES

_____

_____

_____

_____

_____

_____

_____

_____

_____

_____

_____

_____

_____

_____

_____

_____

_____

_____

_____

_____

NOTES

_____

_____

_____

_____

_____

_____

_____

_____

_____

_____

_____

_____

_____

_____

_____

_____

_____

_____

_____

_____

NOTES

_____

_____

_____

_____

_____

_____

_____

_____

_____

_____

_____

_____

_____

_____

_____

_____

_____

_____

_____

_____

_____

_____

NOTES

_____
_____
_____
_____
_____
_____
_____
_____
_____
_____
_____
_____
_____
_____
_____
_____
_____
_____
_____
_____
_____

NOTES

_____

_____

_____

_____

_____

_____

_____

_____

_____

_____

_____

_____

_____

_____

_____

_____

_____

_____

_____

NOTES

_____

_____

_____

_____

_____

_____

_____

_____

_____

_____

_____

_____

_____

_____

_____

_____

_____

_____

_____

_____

NOTES

_____
_____
_____
_____
_____
_____
_____
_____
_____
_____
_____
_____
_____
_____
_____
_____
_____
_____
_____
_____
_____

NOTES

_____

_____

_____

_____

_____

_____

_____

_____

_____

_____

_____

_____

_____

_____

_____

_____

_____

_____

CHAPTER NINE

MISSOURI

ALF BOLIN

ALF BOLIN

The Parable of the Good Samaritan tells the story of a bandit and his cohorts that hid behind a wall of rocks along a treacherous trail, leading from Jerusalem to Jericho. As travelers would happen by, they would jump out from behind the rocks and ambush them, stealing all their money. One man, a Jew, was left by these bandits, bleeding and penniless. Several different people were walking along the trail but chose to ignore his cries for help and not come to his aid. Finally, a gentleman from Samaria was on a journey on the trail and saw the injured man. He stopped to help him and paid for all of his care.

Well, Alfred Bolin and his gang seem to have taken their crime ideas straight from the Good Book. But their victims didn't have a good Samaritan to help them. Bolin and his men would perpetuate a robbery exactly as described in the book of Luke.

The region he exploited was called Pine Mountain, and nicknamed Murder Rocks, for obvious reasons. It held a plethora of jagged and jutting rocks that allowed for a most perfect opportunity. There was a cave near the rocks that Bolin used as a landmark to remember where he buried his stashes which were always along the path in front of the cave.

Bolin was, of course, detested throughout the area and many citizens attempted to put an end to his bullying. He did have one friend, however. Mr. Foster of Taney County was sympathetic toward the gang leader and believed he could be redeemed. His wife was not as hopeful. When Mr. Foster left to serve in the Confederate Army, he was soon captured and sentenced to be killed by the Yankees. But one Union soldier who had caught wind of Bolin and their friendship had a better idea. He offered a deal to Mrs. Foster. If she would help catch Bolin, her husband would be released. This was an easy decision for her and she quickly agreed.

The next day, Mrs. Foster had Bolin over for a meal. The Union soldier was also in attendance, disguised as an injured Confederate soldier. As Bolin leaned over to express his concern to the man, the soldier suddenly jumped up, grabbed him and began beating him with the fireplace poker. He was killed and his head was shoved onto a pole in town as an example to his gang members.

His fortune in stolen gold and valuables was never found. It is believed to be buried near his hideout at Murder Rocks. They are a grouping of limestone rocks in St. Francois County, Missouri. To find Pine Mountain, one should take Cedar Street heading south out of Bismarck, Missouri for approximately three miles. Pine Mountain will be on your left.

Who:_____

What:_____

Where:_____

How:_____

Others:_____

Records/Relatives:_____

Tax/Death/Military:_____

Newspapers:_____

    Internet:_____

    Sources:_____

COMMENTS:_____

_____

_____

_____

_____

_____

_____

_____

_____

_____

Who:_____

What:_____

Where:_____

How:_____

Others:_____

Records/Relatives:_____

Tax/Death/Military:_____

Newspapers:_____

Internet:_____

Sources:_____

COMMENTS:_____

_____

_____

_____

_____

_____

_____

_____

_____

_____

Who:_____

What:_____

Where:_____

How:_____

Others:_____

Records/Relatives:_____

Tax/Death/Military:_____

Newspapers:_____

    Internet:_____

    Sources:_____

COMMENTS:_____

_____

_____

_____

_____

_____

_____

_____

_____

_____

Who:_____

What:_____

Where:_____

How:_____

Others:_____

Records/Relatives:_____

Tax/Death/Military:_____

Newspapers:_____

    Internet:_____

    Sources:_____

COMMENTS:_____

_____

_____

_____

_____

_____

_____

_____

_____

Who:_____

What:_____

Where:_____

How:_____

Others:_____

Records/Relatives:_____

Tax/Death/Military:_____

Newspapers:_____

    Internet:_____

    Sources:_____

COMMENTS:_____

_____

_____

_____

_____

_____

_____

_____

_____

_____

_____

Who:_____

What:_____

Where:_____

How:_____

Others:_____

Records/Relatives:_____

Tax/Death/Military:_____

Newspapers:_____

Internet:_____

Sources:_____

COMMENTS:_____

_____

_____

_____

_____

_____

_____

_____

_____

_____

NOTES

_____

_____

_____

_____

_____

_____

_____

_____

_____

_____

_____

_____

_____

_____

_____

_____

_____

_____

_____

_____

_____

_____

_____

_____

NOTES

_____

_____

_____

_____

_____

_____

_____

_____

_____

_____

_____

_____

_____

_____

_____

_____

_____

_____

_____

_____

_____

NOTES

NOTES

_____

_____

_____

_____

_____

_____

_____

_____

_____

_____

_____

_____

_____

_____

_____

_____

_____

_____

_____

_____

_____

NOTES

_____

_____

_____

_____

_____

_____

_____

_____

_____

_____

_____

_____

_____

_____

_____

_____

_____

_____

_____

_____

NOTES

_____
_____
_____
_____
_____
_____
_____
_____
_____
_____
_____
_____
_____
_____
_____
_____
_____
_____
_____

NOTES

_____
_____
_____
_____
_____
_____
_____
_____
_____
_____
_____
_____
_____
_____
_____
_____
_____
_____
_____
_____

NOTES

NOTES

_____
_____
_____
_____
_____
_____
_____
_____
_____
_____
_____
_____
_____
_____
_____
_____
_____
_____
_____
_____

NOTES

_____

_____

_____

_____

_____

_____

_____

_____

_____

_____

_____

_____

_____

_____

_____

_____

_____

_____

_____

_____

_____

_____

CHAPTER TEN

MISSOURI

BONE HILL

BONE HILL

Before the town of Levasy, Missouri was even a town, it was a place of Indian adventure and lost treasure. Its name was Bone Hill, as a not so subtle reference to the buffalo bones that would rot here for years after the Indians would kill and then strip them of all the meat and intestines. The region was a boon for the Indians in their hunting activities and provided much of their meat and sustenance. Years later, this nickname was confirmed by the settlers who hiked the hills and discovered thousands upon thousands of the sun-bleached bones, along with Indian tools and arrows. But Bone Hill would become well-known for more than just the leftover pieces of the Indian's dinner. For over a century, it has hidden a family's fortune in gold.

Several years before the Civil War, a family moved west to operate a farm in the region. They purchased the property around Bone Hill and developed its acreage, plowing the fields along with their slaves. They constructed a custom stone fence along the borders of the entire property. The farming business proceeded well for several years until the onset of the Civil War when conflicts arose about borders and land disagreements were hotly contested. To solve some of the conflict, the farmer decided to just sell his property and take the money for it. He sold all of the land for a handsome profit and received his payment in gold. Because of the impending war and the precarious state of security during that time, the farmer buried his entire fortune underground along the stone wall.

Although they were disheartened to leave their wonderful neighbors, the family moved west and promised to return in seven years. The father felt that would be enough time for the region, and the country, to work out its conflicts and it would be a safe time to retrieve his funds. The family never returned to Bone Hill, but a mystery has existed ever since their departure.

Exactly seven years to the day, a long and piercing white light appeared and shone on the region, hovering over the stone wall. If it had only occurred that one time, it would have been dismissed as an apparition; however, every seven years since then it has appeared again. The legend explains that the light is now the ghost of the farmer returning to protect and/or lead to his gold fortune. Because of this story that appeared in the state newspaper in the late 1800s, some individuals in the region come together every seven years to wait at the site and catch a glimpse of the famous light.

The most recent seven year period ended in 2009, which means the next sighting will occur in 2016. The stone wall is situated just south of Levasy, Missouri, 1.5 miles west of H Highway, in Jackson County. Levasy is located only twenty miles east of Kansas City, Missouri.

Who:_____

What:_____

Where:_____

How:_____

Others:_____

Records/Relatives:_____

Tax/Death/Military:_____

Newspapers:_____

Internet:_____

Sources:_____

COMMENTS:_____

_____

_____

_____

_____

_____

_____

_____

_____

Who:_____

What:_____

Where:_____

How:_____

Others:_____

Records/Relatives:_____

Tax/Death/Military:_____

Newspapers:_____

Internet:_____

Sources:_____

COMMENTS:_____

_____

_____

_____

_____

_____

_____

_____

_____

_____

Who:_____

What:_____

Where:_____

How:_____

Others:_____

Records/Relatives:_____

Tax/Death/Military:_____

Newspapers:_____

    Internet:_____

    Sources:_____

COMMENTS:_____

_____

_____

_____

_____

_____

_____

_____

_____

_____

Who:_____

What:_____

Where:_____

How:_____

Others:_____

Records/Relatives:_____

Tax/Death/Military:_____

Newspapers:_____

    Internet:_____

    Sources:_____

COMMENTS:_____

_____

_____

_____

_____

_____

_____

_____

_____

_____

Who:_____

What:_____

Where:_____

How:_____

Others:_____

Records/Relatives:_____

Tax/Death/Military:_____

Newspapers:_____

    Internet:_____

    Sources:_____

COMMENTS:_____

_____

_____

_____

_____

_____

_____

_____

_____

_____

Who:_____

What:_____

Where:_____

How:_____

Others:_____

Records/Relatives:_____

Tax/Death/Military:_____

Newspapers:_____

  Internet:_____

  Sources:_____

COMMENTS:_____

_____
_____
_____
_____
_____
_____
_____
_____
_____

NOTES

_____
_____
_____
_____
_____
_____
_____
_____
_____
_____
_____
_____
_____
_____
_____
_____
_____
_____
_____
_____

NOTES

NOTES

_____
_____
_____
_____
_____
_____
_____
_____
_____
_____
_____
_____
_____
_____
_____
_____
_____
_____
_____
_____

NOTES

_____
_____
_____
_____
_____
_____
_____
_____
_____
_____
_____
_____
_____
_____
_____
_____
_____
_____
_____
_____
_____

NOTES

_____

_____

_____

_____

_____

_____

_____

_____

_____

_____

_____

_____

_____

_____

_____

_____

_____

_____

NOTES

NOTES

_____

_____

_____

_____

_____

_____

_____

_____

_____

_____

_____

_____

_____

_____

_____

_____

_____

_____

_____

_____

_____

_____

NOTES

NOTES

_____

_____

_____

_____

_____

_____

_____

_____

_____

_____

_____

_____

_____

_____

_____

_____

_____

_____

_____

_____

_____

NOTES

CHAPTER ELEVEN

MISSOURI

COPPER AXE CAVE

COPPER AXE CAVE

There is a hidden cave in the far southwestern corner of Missouri that has been missing for centuries. It is believed to hold an ancient gold mine worth millions of dollars.

Its discovery began with the expedition of a Spanish man who had gained knowledge of many hidden gold mines in America. He had even obtained maps to back them up. Indians had traded this information with the Spanish prospector who received over two hundred maps, crudely drawn on sheepskin material. However rough the sketches, they were enough to lead the Spaniard to the outskirts of Jane, Missouri and to an amazing find.

He arrived in the region and needed to find the specific cave on the map. After asking several residents, he found a family willing to let him rent a room in their home. Ironically, it was a farmer who had just finished a pitiful season and was short on funds for his expenses. The extra income from a boarder was exactly what they needed at that time. The Spaniard met with the farmer and his wife to discuss their ideas about the location of the mysterious cave from his map. They immediately knew of the cave which he spoke and provided the easy instructions for its access.

The very next morning, the Spaniard was found at the cave, working inside to gather as much gold as possible. He spent several months there at which point he had collected two carpetbags full of gold ore. As a thank you for their assistance, the Spaniard left the map with the farmer before leaving town for good. Before long, the money-strapped farmer and his son were in the cave, working for several weeks. When curious neighbors requested information about what was in the cave, the only thing that the farmer would show them was an old copper Indian axe. They never witnessed anything else being removed or talked about. Before long, the family had packed up all their belongings and left the region, moving to California.

The extensive description of the cave from the map was as follows. There was a cave in the side of a hill on a country road, its entrance concealed by a double layer of rock. In that layer is a small opening, high up on the side of a steep hill. The side of the hill was covered completely with pieces of limestone and flint. Once inside the small entrance, there was an Indian-crafted ladder leading down a narrow shaft. The ladder was fashioned from tree limbs and thick branches. At the bottom of the shaft was a tiny round opening in the rock. At this opening was a thick vein of free gold quartz.

Continuing through the opening led to an open room covered in moist red clay. The room opened into a tunnel which was over two hundred feet in length. Throughout the walls of the tunnel were markings of veins of gold that had been worked, but still contained much ore.

The cave has been hidden since the farmer and his family left for California. It is believed to have many more pounds of gold ore in its mysterious tunnel. The reason it has remained missing for so long is due to the nebulous directions that were recorded on the Spaniard's map. It explained that one should take the highway north from Bentonville, Arkansas heading to Jane, Missouri and cross the state line. Then proceed three miles north on a country road leading east from the highway.

Who:_____

What:_____

Where:_____

How:_____

Others:_____

Records/Relatives:_____

Tax/Death/Military:_____

Newspapers:_____

    Internet:_____

    Sources:_____

COMMENTS:_____

_____

_____

_____

_____

_____

_____

_____

_____

_____

Who:_____

What:_____

Where:_____

How:_____

Others:_____

Records/Relatives:_____

Tax/Death/Military:_____

Newspapers:_____

  Internet:_____

  Sources:_____

COMMENTS:_____

_____

_____

_____

_____

_____

_____

_____

_____

Who:_____

What:_____

Where:_____

How:_____

Others:_____

Records/Relatives:_____

Tax/Death/Military:_____

Newspapers:_____

    Internet:_____

    Sources:_____

COMMENTS:_____

_____

_____

_____

_____

_____

_____

_____

_____

_____

Who:_____

What:_____

Where:_____

How:_____

Others:_____

Records/Relatives:_____

Tax/Death/Military:_____

Newspapers:_____

    Internet:_____

    Sources:_____

COMMENTS:_____

_____

_____

_____

_____

_____

_____

_____

_____

_____

Who:_____

What:_____

Where:_____

How:_____

Others:_____

Records/Relatives:_____

Tax/Death/Military:_____

Newspapers:_____

    Internet:_____

    Sources:_____

COMMENTS:_____

_____

_____

_____

_____

_____

_____

_____

Who:_____

What:_____

Where:_____

How:_____

Others:_____

Records/Relatives:_____

Tax/Death/Military:_____

Newspapers:_____

   Internet:_____

   Sources:_____

COMMENTS:_____

_____

_____

_____

_____

_____

_____

_____

_____

_____

NOTES

_____

_____

_____

_____

_____

_____

_____

_____

_____

_____

_____

_____

_____

_____

_____

_____

_____

_____

_____

_____

_____

NOTES

_____
_____
_____
_____
_____
_____
_____
_____
_____
_____
_____
_____
_____
_____
_____
_____
_____
_____
_____

NOTES

_____
_____
_____
_____
_____
_____
_____
_____
_____
_____
_____
_____
_____
_____
_____
_____
_____
_____
_____

NOTES

_____
_____
_____
_____
_____
_____
_____
_____
_____
_____
_____
_____
_____
_____
_____
_____
_____
_____

NOTES

_____

_____

_____

_____

_____

_____

_____

_____

_____

_____

_____

_____

_____

_____

_____

_____

_____

_____

_____

_____

_____

NOTES

NOTES

_____

_____

_____

_____

_____

_____

_____

_____

_____

_____

_____

_____

_____

_____

_____

_____

_____

_____

_____

_____

_____

NOTES

_____

_____

_____

_____

_____

_____

_____

_____

_____

_____

_____

_____

_____

_____

_____

_____

_____

_____

_____

_____

NOTES

_____
_____
_____
_____
_____
_____
_____
_____
_____
_____
_____
_____
_____
_____
_____
_____
_____
_____
_____
_____
_____
_____

NOTES

_____

_____

_____

_____

_____

_____

_____

_____

_____

_____

_____

_____

_____

_____

_____

_____

_____

_____

_____

CHAPTER TWELVE

MISSOURI

QUANTRILL'S RAIDERS

QUANTRILL'S RAIDERS

At the outbreak of the Civil War, William Clarke Quantrill and his brothers joined the Confederacy, in a veiled attempt to disguise their real goal of looting, plundering, and even murdering people for their money.

Quantrill was actually the leader of a gang, headquartered in Missouri and Kansas during the late 1800s. He and the gang were nicknamed Quantrill's Raiders and when they died, they left a now century-old mystery behind.

Known as some of the fiercest and most brutal attackers in the Midwest, Quantrill and his band of thieves soon tired of their official Confederate duties. He believed the commanders were not tough enough against the Yankees, and he also desperately despised being under someone's authority. He pulled out from official duty and began his own gang of bandits, using the Confederacy as a façade for their crimes. Quantrill ran raids against Union soldiers, robbed homes, attacked boats on the Missouri River, and eventually grew his gang of guerillas to over one hundred members.

Quantrill's Raiders were a vicious bunch, including the likes of Jesse and Frank James and the Younger Brothers. The culmination of their brutal attacks occurred in August of 1863 when the now five hundred member gang headed into Lawrence, Kansas and burned the town to the ground, killing one hundred and fifty men. Throughout the ordeal, his gang looted and plundered through almost every home in the town, collecting a fortune in gold, silver, and other valuables. They fled east to Missouri as the Union Army authorities had gained their bearing and began to strike back. Once they arrived near the town of Independence, Missouri, the raiders buried their overly large stash to protect if from the pursuers and dig it up at a future time. That day would never come.

Most of the gang, and Quantrill himself, were killed after the Kansas attack, leaving the mysterious hoard behind with a legend to follow. For years following the attack, treasure hunters and historians centered their efforts on the Independence, Missouri region, digging and searching for any clues to the treasure's location. Nothing was ever found, until one man felt that he may have gotten close based on the condition of the soil as he began digging. As he described, the ground seemed "different and uneven" and just when the excitement began to build, an apparition of soldiers appeared, surrounding him. According to his report, they blocked the site and wouldn't let him pass. Still others reported flashes of light appearing as warning when they began to dig too close. If they continued, they felt jolts of sparks like lightning course through their bodies. The legend was begun that Quantrill and his Raiders were somehow guarding the buried gold from the grave via their ghosts.

The mysterious gold treasure of Quantrill and his Raiders has never been discovered. There are no recent stories of people getting close and being visited by his spirit, probably because most treasure hunters have been chased away. The site is believed to be on the outskirts of Independence, Missouri, near the Missouri River. It is situated in Jackson County.

Who:_____

What:_____

Where:_____

How:_____

Others:_____

Records/Relatives:_____

Tax/Death/Military:_____

Newspapers:_____

    Internet:_____

    Sources:_____

COMMENTS:_____

_____

_____

_____

_____

_____

_____

_____

_____

_____

Who:_____

What:_____

Where:_____

How:_____

Others:_____

Records/Relatives:_____

Tax/Death/Military:_____

Newspapers:_____

    Internet:_____

    Sources:_____

COMMENTS:_____

_____

_____

_____

_____

_____

_____

_____

_____

_____

_____

Who:_____

What:_____

Where:_____

How:_____

Others:_____

Records/Relatives:_____

Tax/Death/Military:_____

Newspapers:_____

    Internet:_____

    Sources:_____

COMMENTS:_____

_____

_____

_____

_____

_____

_____

_____

_____

_____

Who:_____

What:_____

Where:_____

How:_____

Others:_____

Records/Relatives:_____

Tax/Death/Military:_____

Newspapers:_____

    Internet:_____

    Sources:_____

COMMENTS:_____

_____

_____

_____

_____

_____

_____

_____

_____

Who:_____

What:_____

Where:_____

How:_____

Others:_____

Records/Relatives:_____

Tax/Death/Military:_____

Newspapers:_____

    Internet:_____

    Sources:_____

COMMENTS:_____

_____

_____

_____

_____

_____

_____

_____

_____

Who:_____

What:_____

Where:_____

How:_____

Others:_____

Records/Relatives:_____

Tax/Death/Military:_____

Newspapers:_____

    Internet:_____

    Sources:_____

COMMENTS:_____

_____

_____

_____

_____

_____

_____

_____

_____

_____

NOTES

_____

_____

_____

_____

_____

_____

_____

_____

_____

_____

_____

_____

_____

_____

_____

_____

_____

_____

NOTES

NOTES

_____

_____

_____

_____

_____

_____

_____

_____

_____

_____

_____

_____

_____

_____

_____

_____

_____

_____

_____

NOTES

NOTES

_____

_____

_____

_____

_____

_____

_____

_____

_____

_____

_____

_____

_____

_____

_____

_____

_____

NOTES

_____

_____

_____

_____

_____

_____

_____

_____

_____

_____

_____

_____

_____

_____

_____

_____

_____

_____

_____

NOTES

_____
_____
_____
_____
_____
_____
_____
_____
_____
_____
_____
_____
_____
_____
_____
_____
_____
_____
_____
_____

NOTES

_____

_____

_____

_____

_____

_____

_____

_____

_____

_____

_____

_____

_____

_____

_____

_____

_____

_____

NOTES

_____
_____
_____
_____
_____
_____
_____
_____
_____
_____
_____
_____
_____
_____
_____
_____
_____
_____
_____
_____

NOTES

_____

_____

_____

_____

_____

_____

_____

_____

_____

_____

_____

_____

_____

_____

_____

_____

_____

_____

_____

_____

_____

CHAPTER THIRTEEN

MISSOURI

VALENTINE'S DAY GOLD

171

VALENTINE'S DAY GOLD

Throughout the 1800s, America was the victim of vicious attacks. The reason they were so vicious was because they were committed by people who had no qualms about shooting someone directly in the face in broad daylight, as they cried out for mercy. These perpetrators could kill a mother in cold blood right in front of her children. Not one ounce of compassion was ever found in their blood; they truly were created from a different mold. Instead of love, only greed and envy coursed through their veins. They were the bank robbers of the Midwest.

On Valentine's Day 1866, a day chosen specifically by the bandits, a gang of twelve men rode into the town of Liberty, Missouri. The small town was about to witness the worst robbery in its history. Appearing nonchalant, and in various disguises, the gang members casually strolled outside the Clay County Savings Association Bank while two of their own walked inside. The outlaws quickly jumped the counter, each holding a loaded pistol into the temple of the cashier and his son. Mr. Bird was forced to hand over the entire contents of the safe, $72,000 in gold coins, or be shot dead. As soon as the money had changed hands, the dozen robbers fled the scene.

Laughing amongst themselves at the ease of their crime, the men rode off into the distance north of town. A boy outside the bank was walking to school for the day and cried out, "The bank was robbed!" He was immediately shot and killed by the departing thieves. The authorities were on the trail within seconds, but lost the scent once the gang had entered the surrounding forests. They scanned the region for hours, but were never able to get another lead as to their location.

The lead bandit in the horseback escape was carrying the sacks of gold. As all of the men had split up to confuse the search, they had set a rendezvous point for a certain time. The bandit carrying the gold decided to attempt to double cross his comrades. While they rode north out of Liberty, this one headed west. He buried the entire amount in the forest and then planned to disappear for awhile, returning later after the chaos had abated to recover the loot. Alas, his plan did not work. When he missed the rendezvous, the gang split up and tracked him down. He was immediately killed and the gold was never found.

This gang was so elusive that historians have never been able to pinpoint who actually committed the crime. For many years, locals attributed the robbery to the James and Younger Brothers, but there was never any proof or evidence to that fact.

The treasure is still missing today and believed to be buried west of Liberty in a forested area.

The stolen $72,000 in gold coins is worth $4.5m.

Who:_____

What:_____

Where:_____

How:_____

Others:_____

Records/Relatives:_____

Tax/Death/Military:_____

Newspapers:_____

    Internet:_____

    Sources:_____

COMMENTS:_____

_____

_____

_____

_____

_____

_____

_____

_____

_____

Who:_____

What:_____

Where:_____

How:_____

Others:_____

Records/Relatives:_____

Tax/Death/Military:_____

Newspapers:_____

    Internet:_____

    Sources:_____

COMMENTS:_____

_____

_____

_____

_____

_____

_____

_____

_____

Who:_____

What:_____

Where:_____

How:_____

Others:_____

Records/Relatives:_____

Tax/Death/Military:_____

Newspapers:_____

    Internet:_____

    Sources:_____

COMMENTS:_____

_____

_____

_____

_____

_____

_____

_____

_____

_____

Who:_____

What:_____

Where:_____

How:_____

Others:_____

Records/Relatives:_____

Tax/Death/Military:_____

Newspapers:_____

    Internet:_____

    Sources:_____

COMMENTS:_____

_____

_____

_____

_____

_____

_____

_____

_____

Who:_____

What:_____

Where:_____

How:_____

Others:_____

Records/Relatives:_____

Tax/Death/Military:_____

Newspapers:_____

    Internet:_____

    Sources:_____

COMMENTS:_____

_____

_____

_____

_____

_____

_____

_____

_____

Who:_____

What:_____

Where:_____

How:_____

Others:_____

Records/Relatives:_____

Tax/Death/Military:_____

Newspapers:_____

    Internet:_____

    Sources:_____

COMMENTS:_____

_____

_____

_____

_____

_____

_____

_____

_____

NOTES

NOTES

_____

_____

_____

_____

_____

_____

_____

_____

_____

_____

_____

_____

_____

_____

_____

_____

_____

NOTES

NOTES

_____
_____
_____
_____
_____
_____
_____
_____
_____
_____
_____
_____
_____
_____
_____
_____
_____
_____
_____
_____
_____

NOTES

_____
_____
_____
_____
_____
_____
_____
_____
_____
_____
_____
_____
_____
_____
_____
_____
_____
_____
_____
_____
_____

NOTES

_____

_____

_____

_____

_____

_____

_____

_____

_____

_____

_____

_____

_____

_____

_____

_____

_____

_____

_____

NOTES

_____

_____

_____

_____

_____

_____

_____

_____

_____

_____

_____

_____

_____

_____

_____

_____

_____

_____

_____

_____

NOTES

NOTES

_____

_____

_____

_____

_____

_____

_____

_____

_____

_____

_____

_____

_____

_____

_____

_____

_____

_____

_____

_____

_____

189

NOTES

CHAPTER FOURTEEN

MISSOURI

LIVINGSTON LEAD

LIVINGSTON LEAD

For one American, the ability to be flexible and change plans based on new information would prove to be a very profitable characteristic in his life. Making a last minute decision when heading for a planned goal can be difficult, but at times it is necessary.

Take, for example, the case of Thomas Livingston. He had organized and dreamed for over a year of traveling to California to join in on the gold rush. When personal responsibilities did not allow for it in his schedule, he bided his time and kept the dream in his heart alive. Day after day, he continued in his daily duties but thought about the land to the west.

Eventually, the timing was right and he gathered his small team together to make the trip. They had only gotten as far as Missouri when they met up with a large group of prospectors returning from a year long visit to California. The prospectors shared many distressing stories about their failures at the gold mines and how they now had barely enough money to make it home. Story after story continued, and the entire group, consisting of hundreds of men, was traveling east with not one gold nugget to its name.

Livingston was faced with a decision to make. He knew there was gold in California, he had heard reports for over a year attesting to that fact. But the truth in the men's eyes told a different story. Surely it would be a risk to continue, a risk he wasn't willing to take. In a stroke of fate, Livingston heard of the possibility of lead in the immediate vicinity of their camp. He decided to keep the group back and find the lead instead of searching for gold.

His decision turned out to be a good one, as the lead was abundant and priced high for the time period. He discovered a rich vein of lead almost immediately and set up his own lead mine, with one hundred workers. The region was nicknamed Minersville and quickly grew to a moderate size. They continued for several years, and Livingston brought in great profits to his business. The mine was recorded as bringing in over thirty million dollars of lead during its existence.

Soon, rumors of a civil war became more than rumors and the country was on the brink of a massive conflict. Livingston knew that the battles would include looting and pillaging and so he decided to close down the mine. He commanded everyone to take their belongings and flee the area before they were robbed by Union soldiers.

Livingston himself had savings of over $10,000 in gold coins from the strong year of profits. He buried it on his property and then took to the woods to hide out from the Union soldiers. He never returned for his family, or the buried gold cache. To this day, it is still missing. It is believed to be buried somewhere on his former property which was west of Carthage, Missouri, in Jasper County.

The $10,000 in gold coins today is valued at $625,000.

Who:_____

What:_____

Where:_____

How:_____

Others:_____

Records/Relatives:_____

Tax/Death/Military:_____

Newspapers:_____

    Internet:_____

    Sources:_____

COMMENTS:_____

_____

_____

_____

_____

_____

_____

_____

_____

_____

Who:_____

What:_____

Where:_____

How:_____

Others:_____

Records/Relatives:_____

Tax/Death/Military:_____

Newspapers:_____

    Internet:_____

    Sources:_____

COMMENTS:_____

_____

_____

_____

_____

_____

_____

_____

_____

Who:_____

What:_____

Where:_____

How:_____

Others:_____

Records/Relatives:_____

Tax/Death/Military:_____

Newspapers:_____

    Internet:_____

    Sources:_____

COMMENTS:_____

_____

_____

_____

_____

_____

_____

_____

_____

Who:_____

What:_____

Where:_____

How:_____

Others:_____

Records/Relatives:_____

Tax/Death/Military:_____

Newspapers:_____

   Internet:_____

   Sources:_____

COMMENTS:_____

_____

_____

_____

_____

_____

_____

_____

_____

_____

Who:_____

What:_____

Where:_____

How:_____

Others:_____

Records/Relatives:_____

Tax/Death/Military:_____

Newspapers:_____

    Internet:_____

    Sources:_____

COMMENTS:_____

_____

_____

_____

_____

_____

_____

_____

_____

_____

Who:_____

What:_____

Where:_____

How:_____

Others:_____

Records/Relatives:_____

Tax/Death/Military:_____

Newspapers:_____

    Internet:_____

    Sources:_____

COMMENTS:_____

_____

_____

_____

_____

_____

_____

_____

_____

NOTES

_____

_____

_____

_____

_____

_____

_____

_____

_____

_____

_____

_____

_____

_____

_____

_____

_____

_____

_____

_____

_____

NOTES

NOTES

_____

_____

_____

_____

_____

_____

_____

_____

_____

_____

_____

_____

_____

_____

_____

_____

_____

_____

_____

_____

NOTES

_____

_____

_____

_____

_____

_____

_____

_____

_____

_____

_____

_____

_____

_____

_____

_____

_____

_____

_____

_____

NOTES

_____

_____

_____

_____

_____

_____

_____

_____

_____

_____

_____

_____

_____

_____

_____

_____

_____

_____

_____

NOTES

_____

_____

_____

_____

_____

_____

_____

_____

_____

_____

_____

_____

_____

_____

_____

_____

_____

_____

_____

_____

_____

NOTES

NOTES

_____
_____
_____
_____
_____
_____
_____
_____
_____
_____
_____
_____
_____
_____
_____
_____
_____
_____
_____

NOTES

_____
_____
_____
_____
_____
_____
_____
_____
_____
_____
_____
_____
_____
_____
_____
_____
_____
_____
_____
_____
_____

NOTES

CHAPTER FIFTEEN

MISSOURI

LOST BUCKET OF GOLD

LOST BUCKET OF GOLD

In 1925, a farm hand would experience a night of adventure he would never forget. Ellis Trent was working in Louisiana for a farmer, helping with the daily chores. As part of his payment, he was permitted to sleep in the barn with the animals. Having a roof over his head and soft hay to sleep in was all that Ellis needed to be content and he was thankful for his makeshift home.

One night, he was awakened from a deep sleep by several gunshots and the unmistakable sound of galloping horses heading toward the barn. Suddenly, a trio of robbers dove into the barn to hideout from the pursuing authorities. Ellis remained hidden behind the hay bales so they would not see him. After laying still for a couple of minutes, the bandits began speaking to one another and decided to bury the loot under the hay and come back later the next morning to retrieve it. Ellis watched carefully as they hid their stash and then fled the scene. He looked at this situation as his big break. Once he was sure that they were definitely off of the property, he dug out the large bucket and left for his home in Huzzah, Missouri.

As he walked off the property and started on his journey he came to a realization. Both the posse and the outlaws would soon be up, looking for the gold. He didn't want to face either group's wrath. Ellis quickened his pace but struggled greatly with both the weight of the bucket and its awkward carrying handle. Because he was trying to avoid the busy paths and any people that might be out, he remained in the woods, crossing ice filled stream and taking no time to sleep. Before long his body felt weary and ill, but he pressed on.

The long trip, coupled with no food and no sleep, left Ellis severely ill. He contracted pneumonia and was filled with utter weakness. The bucket felt like a lead weight around his neck, so he dragged it to the side of the trail and buried it underground. He was only three miles from home at this point, and somehow he managed to eventually arrive. Ellis' family immediately put him to bed and called the local doctor. But before he was able to schedule a medical visit, Ellis had slipped further into a subconscious state. He summoned his brother over to the bed and told him the story about the barn and the bucket of gold. He confided in him also about the location where it was buried.

When he was just three miles from his home, he stopped by a spring to get a drink of water and there he found a large shelter rock. Next to the rock was a fox's hole in which he placed the bucket, covering it up with small stones.

Ellis died before morning came, and his family headed to the area later on to look for his buried bucket. They were unable to find the shelter rock, the fox's hole, or the bucket of gold. The gold today is expected to be buried somewhere three miles south of Huzzah, Missouri. The entire area is covered by Mark Twain National Forest which has several streams within its covering. One of these Crawford County streams is lying next to a fortune in gold.

Who:_____

What:_____

Where:_____

How:_____

Others:_____

Records/Relatives:_____

Tax/Death/Military:_____

Newspapers:_____

    Internet:_____

    Sources:_____

COMMENTS:_____

_____

_____

_____

_____

_____

_____

_____

_____

_____

Who:_____

What:_____

Where:_____

How:_____

Others:_____

Records/Relatives:_____

Tax/Death/Military:_____

Newspapers:_____

    Internet:_____

    Sources:_____

COMMENTS:_____

_____

_____

_____

_____

_____

_____

_____

_____

_____

Who:_____

What:_____

Where:_____

How:_____

Others:_____

Records/Relatives:_____

Tax/Death/Military:_____

Newspapers:_____

    Internet:_____

    Sources:_____

COMMENTS:_____

_____

_____

_____

_____

_____

_____

_____

_____

_____

Who:_____

What:_____

Where:_____

How:_____

Others:_____

Records/Relatives:_____

Tax/Death/Military:_____

Newspapers:_____

    Internet:_____

    Sources:_____

COMMENTS:_____

_____

_____

_____

_____

_____

_____

_____

_____

Who:_____

What:_____

Where:_____

How:_____

Others:_____

Records/Relatives:_____

Tax/Death/Military:_____

Newspapers:_____

    Internet:_____

    Sources:_____

COMMENTS:_____

_____

_____

_____

_____

_____

_____

_____

_____

_____

Who:_____

What:_____

Where:_____

How:_____

Others:_____

Records/Relatives:_____

Tax/Death/Military:_____

Newspapers:_____

    Internet:_____

    Sources:_____

COMMENTS:_____

_____

_____

_____

_____

_____

_____

_____

_____

_____

NOTES

_____
_____
_____
_____
_____
_____
_____
_____
_____
_____
_____
_____
_____
_____
_____
_____
_____
_____
_____

NOTES

NOTES

_____

_____

_____

_____

_____

_____

_____

_____

_____

_____

_____

_____

_____

_____

_____

_____

_____

_____

_____

NOTES

NOTES

_____
_____
_____
_____
_____
_____
_____
_____
_____
_____
_____
_____
_____
_____
_____
_____
_____
_____
_____

NOTES

_____

_____

_____

_____

_____

_____

_____

_____

_____

_____

_____

_____

_____

_____

_____

_____

_____

_____

_____

NOTES

_____

_____

_____

_____

_____

_____

_____

_____

_____

_____

_____

_____

_____

_____

_____

_____

_____

_____

_____

NOTES

_____

_____

_____

_____

_____

_____

_____

_____

_____

_____

_____

_____

_____

_____

_____

_____

_____

_____

_____

_____

_____

_____

NOTES

_____
_____
_____
_____
_____
_____
_____
_____
_____
_____
_____
_____
_____
_____
_____
_____
_____
_____

NOTES

_____
_____
_____
_____
_____
_____
_____
_____
_____
_____
_____
_____
_____
_____
_____
_____
_____
_____
_____

CHAPTER SIXTEEN

MISSOURI

FRED'S FARM CACHE

FRED'S FARM CACHE

One of the most terrifying gangsters in the history of the Midwest was Fred Burke. Along with a small gang that changed members frequently, Fred had robbed banks and individuals for several years, amassing a total of $100,000 in gold coins. After hearing from his mother one day about how proud she was of him and his success in life (she had no idea about his true identity or career), he felt overwhelmed with a sense of guilt and shame. Fred decided that he wanted to live a normal and legal life, following the rules just like all the other citizens. A side reason, and a quite compelling one at that, was that Fred knew the authorities were on his trail and it wouldn't be long before his capture and demise.

He informed his contacts in the gangster community that he was leaving the region, changing his name, and would be an honest citizen from that point on. Although they were extremely skeptical, the other bandits bid him farewell and good luck. Secretly, they were happy about his announcement because it would mean more loot and opportunities for them.

Fred's first stop on his new life's journey was at a farm in Green City, Missouri. He requested a job as a farm hand and was readily accepted, although he had no experience. Once he had learned the ropes, he packaged up his small fortune into five separate packages of $20,000 in each. One package he kept on his person for expenses, but he buried the other four on the farm, certain that the farmer would never be wise to his secret.

His new life took its second step when he married the farmer's daughter and began to serve in the community. It seemed that he had truly become a different person. But these changes were all by outward appearances and evidently not in his heart. Fred was still a very angry individual and he had suppressed it for long enough. On the way to Michigan to pick up farm equipment for his father-in-law, he was stopped by police for a minor infraction. This set off his temper and he shot the policeman before fleeing the scene.

There was an immediate picture of Fred in every post office and courthouse in the Midwest. One of his neighbors noticed the wanted ads and called the police, alerting them to his presence on the farm. They soon swarmed the property, arresting him and serving him a life sentence in a Michigan prison. His one act of rage had cost him his wife, his job, his buried gold, and his new life.

Fred remained in prison until his death and never revealed to anyone the secret location of his gold. It remains hidden underground at a farm on the outskirts of Green City, Missouri, in Sullivan County.

Who:_____

What:_____

Where:_____

How:_____

Others:_____

Records/Relatives:_____

Tax/Death/Military:_____

Newspapers:_____

    Internet:_____

    Sources:_____

COMMENTS:_____

_____

_____

_____

_____

_____

_____

_____

_____

_____

Who:_____

What:_____

Where:_____

How:_____

Others:_____

Records/Relatives:_____

Tax/Death/Military:_____

Newspapers:_____

    Internet:_____

    Sources:_____

COMMENTS:_____

_____

_____

_____

_____

_____

_____

_____

_____

_____

Who:_____

What:_____

Where:_____

How:_____

Others:_____

Records/Relatives:_____

Tax/Death/Military:_____

Newspapers:_____

    Internet:_____

    Sources:_____

COMMENTS:_____

_____

_____

_____

_____

_____

_____

_____

_____

Who:_____

What:_____

Where:_____

How:_____

Others:_____

Records/Relatives:_____

Tax/Death/Military:_____

Newspapers:_____

    Internet:_____

    Sources:_____

COMMENTS:_____

_____

_____

_____

_____

_____

_____

_____

_____

_____

Who:_____

What:_____

Where:_____

How:_____

Others:_____

Records/Relatives:_____

Tax/Death/Military:_____

Newspapers:_____

    Internet:_____

    Sources:_____

COMMENTS:_____

_____

_____

_____

_____

_____

_____

_____

_____

_____

_____

Who:_____

What:_____

Where:_____

How:_____

Others:_____

Records/Relatives:_____

Tax/Death/Military:_____

Newspapers:_____

    Internet:_____

    Sources:_____

COMMENTS:_____

_____

_____

_____

_____

_____

_____

_____

_____

NOTES

_____
_____
_____
_____
_____
_____
_____
_____
_____
_____
_____
_____
_____
_____
_____
_____
_____
_____
_____
_____
_____

NOTES

_____
_____
_____
_____
_____
_____
_____
_____
_____
_____
_____
_____
_____
_____
_____
_____
_____
_____
_____
_____

NOTES

_____
_____
_____
_____
_____
_____
_____
_____
_____
_____
_____
_____
_____
_____
_____
_____
_____
_____
_____
_____
_____

NOTES

_____
_____
_____
_____
_____
_____
_____
_____
_____
_____
_____
_____
_____
_____
_____
_____
_____
_____
_____
_____
_____

NOTES

_____

_____

_____

_____

_____

_____

_____

_____

_____

_____

_____

_____

_____

_____

_____

_____

_____

_____

NOTES

_____
_____
_____
_____
_____
_____
_____
_____
_____
_____
_____
_____
_____
_____
_____
_____
_____
_____
_____
_____
_____
_____
_____

NOTES

_____

_____

_____

_____

_____

_____

_____

_____

_____

_____

_____

_____

_____

_____

_____

_____

_____

_____

_____

_____

_____

NOTES

_____

_____

_____

_____

_____

_____

_____

_____

_____

_____

_____

_____

_____

_____

_____

_____

_____

_____

NOTES

_____

_____

_____

_____

_____

_____

_____

_____

_____

_____

_____

_____

_____

_____

_____

_____

_____

_____

_____

_____

NOTES

CHAPTER SEVENTEEN

MISSOURI

A DOCTOR'S BETRAYAL

A DOCTOR'S BETRAYAL

A doctor in Nodaway County, Missouri faced the ultimate betrayal in his life; a betrayal by his own flesh and blood.

After the Civil War, Doctor Lynn Talbott moved to Barnard, Missouri to open up a practice in the small but quaint town. He became quite popular and was highly sought after for his medical advice. Because of his large number of patients and a constantly busy workload, Talbott became wealthy and decided to build a bigger home just north of town. He chose an area on the stagecoach road and bought many acres. The house was constructed by his own design and was called the House of the Seven Gables. It was a perfect home for him and his wife and their two sons. There was one additional houseguest their servant.

Talbott's sons, Charles and Hugh, grew resentful over time of all the hours their father put into caring for other children and their families, yet all the while ignoring them. He was what would be described today as a workaholic.

His profits multiplied rapidly and before long, Talbott was putting his entire pay into savings. This he accomplished by filling up an empty nail keg with five, ten, and twenty dollar gold coins. He continued on for months until the keg was filled to almost overflowing. At that point, he was ready to hide it underground to avoid theft. He did so in the dark of night and was completely unseen. He never told anyone where the money was buried, but his family was aware that it existed.

In 1869, the doctor was reading by the window one evening and was shot with one bullet to the head. His sons, servant, and wife came running in, only to find Talbott lying on the floor with blood pouring from his temple. A quick check confirmed his death, but the questions lingered in the air…why?…how? There were no signs of foul play anywhere to be seen. The sheriff was summoned and he came quickly to the family mansion. The search for clues came up completely empty and provided no information about the doctor's mysterious death.

Finally, the sons were playing outside one day with a good friend and decided to bring him in on their little secret. "We killed our father," they confided, "so we could have all his gold. If you help us look for it, we'll share with you in the profits." The friend was appalled, but played along so as not to become their next victim.

As soon as he was home, he raced to the sheriff's office and told him what the boys had said. Sheriff Toel made a trip out to the ranch and arrested both sons for their father's murder. When pressed for a motive, they explained that they just wanted his gold all for themselves. Ironically, they did not know where the stash was before they killed him. Both boys were sentenced to be hanged because of their heinous crime.

The mother was left alone and depressed. She did a quick scan of most of the property with her eyes and didn't see anything out of the ordinary. It was then that she resigned to her fate as a poor widow and lived out the rest of her years in misery.

The keg of gold was never found and is believed to be buried just north of Barnard, Missouri, in the extreme northwest corner of the state.

Who:_____

What:_____

Where:_____

How:_____

Others:_____

Records/Relatives:_____

Tax/Death/Military:_____

Newspapers:_____

    Internet:_____

    Sources:_____

COMMENTS:_____

_____

_____

_____

_____

_____

_____

_____

_____

_____

Who:_____

What:_____

Where:_____

How:_____

Others:_____

Records/Relatives:_____

Tax/Death/Military:_____

Newspapers:_____

    Internet:_____

    Sources:_____

COMMENTS:_____

_____

_____

_____

_____

_____

_____

_____

_____

_____

Who:_____

What:_____

Where:_____

How:_____

Others:_____

Records/Relatives:_____

Tax/Death/Military:_____

Newspapers:_____

    Internet:_____

    Sources:_____

COMMENTS:_____

_____

_____

_____

_____

_____

_____

_____

_____

_____

_____

Who:_____

What:_____

Where:_____

How:_____

Others:_____

Records/Relatives:_____

Tax/Death/Military:_____

Newspapers:_____

    Internet:_____

    Sources:_____

COMMENTS:_____

_____

_____

_____

_____

_____

_____

_____

_____

Who:_____

What:_____

Where:_____

How:_____

Others:_____

Records/Relatives:_____

Tax/Death/Military:_____

Newspapers:_____

    Internet:_____

    Sources:_____

COMMENTS:_____

_____

_____

_____

_____

_____

_____

_____

_____

_____

Who:_____

What:_____

Where:_____

How:_____

Others:_____

Records/Relatives:_____

Tax/Death/Military:_____

Newspapers:_____

    Internet:_____

    Sources:_____

COMMENTS:_____

_____

_____

_____

_____

_____

_____

_____

_____

_____

NOTES

_____

_____

_____

_____

_____

_____

_____

_____

_____

_____

_____

_____

_____

_____

_____

_____

_____

_____

NOTES

_____

_____

_____

_____

_____

_____

_____

_____

_____

_____

_____

_____

_____

_____

_____

_____

_____

_____

_____

NOTES

_____
_____
_____
_____
_____
_____
_____
_____
_____
_____
_____
_____
_____
_____
_____
_____
_____
_____
_____
_____
_____

NOTES

_____

_____

_____

_____

_____

_____

_____

_____

_____

_____

_____

_____

_____

_____

_____

_____

_____

_____

_____

_____

NOTES

_____

_____

_____

_____

_____

_____

_____

_____

_____

_____

_____

_____

_____

_____

_____

_____

_____

_____

_____

_____

NOTES

_____
_____
_____
_____
_____
_____
_____
_____
_____
_____
_____
_____
_____
_____
_____
_____
_____
_____
_____
_____

NOTES

_____
_____
_____
_____
_____
_____
_____
_____
_____
_____
_____
_____
_____
_____
_____
_____
_____
_____
_____
_____
_____

NOTES

_____

_____

_____

_____

_____

_____

_____

_____

_____

_____

_____

_____

_____

_____

_____

_____

_____

_____

NOTES

_____

_____

_____

_____

_____

_____

_____

_____

_____

_____

_____

_____

_____

_____

_____

_____

NOTES

_____

_____

_____

_____

_____

_____

_____

_____

_____

_____

_____

_____

_____

_____

_____

_____

_____

_____

_____

_____

CPSIA information can be obtained
at www.ICGtesting.com
Printed in the USA
LVHW101236030121
675562LV00035B/784